THE ART OF I. COMPTON-BURNETT

A Collection of Critical Essays

edited by

CHARLES BURKHART

with contributions by:

John Betjeman

Elizabeth Bowen

Charles Burkhart

John Ginger

R. Glynn Grylls

A. Norman Jeffares

Margaret Jourdain

Francis King

Robert Liddell

Michael Millgate

Raymond Mortimer

Anthony Powell

John Preston

Mario Praz

Edward Sackville-West

Nathalie Sarraute

Hilary Spurling

Angus Wilson

LONDON

VICTOR GOLLANCZ LTD

1972

ISBN 0 575 01402 4

Nathalie Sarraute's essay from THE AGE OF SUSPICION
was first published in France under the title L'ere du
Soupçon © Librairie Gallimard 1956

C

Printed in Great Britain by
The Camelot Press Ltd, London and Southampton

CONTENTS

INTRODUCTION

'HONORIS CAUSA.' Ivy Compton-Burnett was awarded the degree of Doctor of Letters, *honoris causa*, by Leeds University in 1960; and here, for the same reason, some twelve years later, appears this first collection of critical essays on her writing. The first item in the collection is Professor Jeffares' introductory speech at the awarding of the degree. It begins with 'Your Royal Highness' (the Princess Royal was present), which seems to me a resounding note, one Dame Ivy would have enjoyed, to commence a volume that is in fact commemorative as well as critical: an intention I have emphasised by placing three well-wrought obituaries—which she would have enjoyed less—at the end of the volume (and even 'collections' should have a shape).

It is time, three years after her death, for some more formal recognition of her great art. There have been full-length critical studies in the past, and more are soon to come; two biographies, by Elizabeth Sprigge and Hilary Spurling, are, to use one of Ivy's expressions, on the stocks. But since no two critics ever quite agree about the twenty novels that began with *Dolores* in 1911 and ended with the posthumous *The Last and the First* half a century later in 1971, to bring together some of their opinions in a single volume may, by the richness of their diversities, indicate the complexities of her art, which on the surface may seem to, and in fact does, have a classical sameness.

As to other purposes: as a source book for future study of the novels, I hope these essays may prove useful. They may suggest directions for enquiry that will increase our understanding of the books; for example, John Preston's linguistic analysis in his comments on *A Heritage and Its History* could very interestingly be broadened to illuminate her work as a whole.

Some of these articles were written by her distinguished fellow-novelists; it is a truism that the practitioner understands the practice best. It has been a pleasure to include deeply thought-out pieces by, for example, Elizabeth Bowen and Angus Wilson. I have tried to collect some of the most interesting criticism on Compton-Burnett—in one volume one cannot of course collect it all.

It has been said that the best criticism of Compton-Burnett has been written by those who do not like her books, or have 'serious reservations' about them; it would be odd if this were often true. The aim of my selection is not a chorus of delight, but a sympathetic and serious dialogue among her critically-gifted admirers.

There are twenty novels by her, and twenty pieces in this book, by a total of eighteen writers (there are two each by the two novelists just mentioned, Elizabeth Bowen and Angus Wilson). There are the general (as Professor Jeffares' speech and the three obituaries would naturally tend towards) and the specific, especially in the third section, a series of short reviews contemporary with the publication of various of the novels. But preceding these seven reviews are placed two basic documents which seem to me an indispensable preface. The first is the famous radio 'Conversation between I. Compton-Burnett and M. Jourdain', recorded in Lyme Regis, where the two friends had gone to escape the bombs. It was published by *Orion* in 1945. It is a sharp and amiable dialogue; everything Ivy says in it is at her most characteristically rational, scrupulous, and humorous; its most profound and most-quoted comment is the following:

> As regards plots I find real life no help at all. Real life seems to have no plots. And as I think a plot desirable and almost necessary, I have this extra grudge against life. But I think there are signs that strange things happen, though they do not emerge. I believe it would go ill with many of us, if we were faced by a strong temptation, and I suspect that with some of us it does go ill.

Grim, for Lyme Regis; but the deeper truths are always grim; and Lyme Regis had also once housed Jane Austen, the writer in no way shallow with whom Ivy Compton-Burnett has most often been compared.

In the interview with Michael Millgate, which follows the *Orion* conversation by fifteen years, many of the ideas remain the same—aspects of her outlook, her tone, her wit. Here is what Professor Millgate has written to me about it:

> The interview took place on Friday, November 20, 1959. I used a tape-recorder and subsequently sent a copy of the transcript to Miss Compton-Burnett, inviting her to make any change she wished. She took me at my word and made extensive revisions, not so much in the content of her remarks (though there were a few interesting additions) as in their phrasing; she also sharpened up some of my questions! As she explained in an accompanying letter, she wanted to save the interview from being 'too colloquial and incoherent'—and now felt, in fact, that it went 'rather well'.

Somehow one *sees* Ivy very vividly in this interview; one sees her prim little figure turning towards a friend, eyes twinkling with expectation as she launched a *mot*: 'I shouldn't mind being described as amoral'—herself chuckling along with her friend's laughter. Professor Millgate questioned her particularly about her actual method of composition, with, as the result, a fascinating account of her creative process. She was both generous and negative about her creative contemporaries; she said that she admired both E. M. Forster and Virginia Woolf, but the former, she said, 'to be quite honest', was 'overestimated'; and she asked Professor Millgate about the latter, 'Well, is she really a novelist?' Also in this interview she rises to one of her rare moments of great personal eloquence:

> I think that the world I draw, that some people say has vanished, will always go on, with certain modifications that must be caused by modern life. I think that human experiences and emotions remain almost the same, and that they have more scope in that sort of set life than in the life of flux that many people lead nowadays. It seems to me that as new worlds arise and pass, the world of my books remains, and that it is getting added to, as richer people, who may come from anywhere, rise up and join it. And I think that people have always done this, and always will.

The seven short reviews which make up a section of their own in this book say a great deal in very little space. Would any collection of criticism on modern British literature be complete

without at least one item by Raymond Mortimer? I have chosen a
very early one, a review of *A House and Its Head* in 1935, which
succeeds, remarkably for that date, in placing the work of this
writer, who seemed a much odder figure then than now; which
evokes the literary climate of that era; which makes the exact and
inevitable comparison of Compton-Burnett with Racine.
Elizabeth Bowen's two review essays (on *Parents and Children*,
1941, and on *Elders and Betters*, 1944) show how the Compton-
Burnett novels are post-Victorian, in the way they continue and
enlarge on some of the Victorian pre-occupations; and there is a
superb image of Dame Ivy's style in a phrase that could only
come from another masterful stylist: '. . . an icy sharpness prevails
in their dialogue. In fact, to read in these days a page of Compton-
Burnett dialogue is to think of the sound of glass being swept up,
one of these London mornings after a blitz.' To follow Miss
Bowen I thought it might be interesting to include two on-the-
spot reviews of one novel, by two of its most alert critics, and I
have placed side by side two notices of *A Father and His Fate*
(1957), that of John Betjeman in the *Daily Telegraph* and that of
R. Glynn Grylls in the *Sunday Times*. It is the latter which fixes
for ever the Compton-Burnett subject in a phrase: 'a family
whose address is "Huis Clos"'. As was already said the review-
essay by John Preston makes use of linguistic analysis, to show
how form and content are essentially the same in a Compton-
Burnett novel; and the final article in this group of reviews is
Hilary Spurling's on *Dolores* and *The Last and the First*, which
brings together the first and the last of the twenty novels.

More extended in scope, more ranging and relating and various,
are the seven essays which follow. With one exception: my own
essay—and it is an essay, in the basic meaning of the word—
which has the limited aim of pointing out a few ways in which
the twenty novels are not the same but different, so that a pattern
to the Compton-Burnett career can tentatively be begun to be set
forth. The most important essay of the seven is probably Robert
Liddell's, an Appendix to his *Treatise on the Novel* of 1947, which,
though a pioneer work in Compton-Burnett study, remains the
authoritative analysis of such matters in her world as tyranny and
violence and the connection between them; which, by its breadth

and perception, substantiates the claim made at the conclusion that 'of all English novelists now writing she is the greatest and the most original artist'. Mr Liddell elaborated ideas from this essay in his full-length study of several years later, *The Novels of I. Compton-Burnett.*★

The essay following Mr Liddell's is Edward Sackville-West's, and it makes a revealing comparison between the novels of Ivy Compton-Burnett and Elizabeth Bowen, one which gains in implication because of the two reviews of Compton-Burnett by Bowen included earlier. Next is Professor Mario Praz, whose essay had not been translated in its entirety before. My own translation of it was greatly aided by my friend Professor Monica Letzring and by Professor Praz himself. One likes this essay because it has the bold historical sweep characteristic of Professor Praz's writing, and because it is so specific on the Greek aspects of Compton-Burnett. It is personal, daring, and exciting. Adventurous in another way is the manifesto by Nathalie Sarraute. Mme Sarraute announces the datedness, indeed the death, of the psychological novel, and theorises on the function of dialogue, of conversation and sub-conversation, in present and future fiction. It is a recurrent idea among her critics, that Compton-Burnett dialogue operates on two levels, of what is said, and what is all the louder for not being said.

Even though, as he has told me, Angus Wilson's views of her novels have somewhat altered since his *London Magazine* piece of 1955 on Compton-Burnett appeared, it retains its importance as an examination of the terms on which she can or cannot be considered a great novelist and of her special resemblances to and differences from Jane Austen, Henry James and Tolstoy. The *London Magazine* essay by John Ginger is quite recent (1970) and can serve as a good modern introduction to her books and their major concerns (religion, self-sacrifice, etc.); for its precision and insight it also fitly serves as a conclusion to this group of large-scale evaluations. Among the three obituaries which finish the volume, Anthony Powell's places Ivy Compton-Burnett historically and culturally; Angus Wilson's makes wide literary claims for her; and Francis King's is the most deeply felt.

★ Gollancz, 1955.

She keenly believed in her own books and hoped for fame; she knew which of her critics she liked, and why; I hope that she would have approved this book, but found cause for both disagreement and agreement with its contents. She would have hoped, as I do, that it would lead more readers to what is more important than this book and its twenty essays, the twenty novels that she wrote.

ACKNOWLEDGEMENTS

AMONG FRIENDS OR students of I. Compton-Burnett I am particularly grateful for help in preparing this book to Herman Schrijver, Lady Mander (R. Glynn Grylls), Livia Gollancz, Elizabeth Sprigge, Hilary Spurling, and Blake Nevius. Many of the contributors to this volume gave very freely of their time and effort, as well as granting me permission to include their pieces, and to all of them my deepest thanks. I am also indebted to:

A. Norman Jeffares for permission to use his speech preceding the award of the honorary doctorate to I. Compton-Burnett;
Rosamond Lehmann, Denys Kilham Roberts, Cecil Day Lewis, Anthony Compton-Burnett, and the Society of Authors for the *Orion* 'Conversation';
A Review of English Literature for Michael Millgate's 'Interview';
The *New Statesman* for Raymond Mortimer's review;
The *New Statesman* and Curtis Brown Ltd for the Elizabeth Bowen reviews;
The *Daily Telegraph* for the John Betjeman review;
The *Sunday Times* for the R. Glynn Grylls review;
Essays in Criticism for the John Preston review;
The *New Statesman* for the Hilary Spurling review;
John Cushman Associates Inc. and Jonathan Cape Ltd for the Robert Liddell essay;
Martin Secker & Warburg Ltd for the Edward Sackville-West essay;
Professor Mario Praz for permission to translate and print 'I romanzi di Ivy Compton-Burnett'; Lady Mander, who brought this essay to my attention; Miss Cantu of the British Council in London and Professor Monica Letzring of Philadelphia for other assistance with this essay;
The *London Magazine* for the Angus Wilson essay;
Calder and Boyars Ltd and George Braziller Inc. for the Nathalie Sarraute essay translated by Maria Jolas;

The *London Magazine* for the John Ginger essay;
The *Spectator* for the obituary by Anthony Powell and C. A. Seaton,
    Librarian of the *Spectator*;
The *Observer* for the obituary by Angus Wilson; and
The *Sunday Telegraph* for the obituary by Francis King.

I

HONORIS CAUSA

A. Norman Jeffares

SPEECH OF INTRODUCTION TO THE AWARDING OF THE DOCTOR OF LETTERS DEGREE, LEEDS UNIVERSITY, MAY 19, 1960

YOUR ROYAL HIGHNESS and Chancellor:

Miss Compton-Burnett has given us some sixteen major novels. She inherits Jane Austen's precise vocabulary and delicately pointed use of it; her plainness of speech is matched by sophisticated understatement. Her style is, then, ironic; her setting is a world based on late nineteenth-century country-house life; and her subject is the tension between human beings, between classes, between the strong and the weak, and between the generations. For all her novels contain characters with modern methods of thought; against complacency, tyranny and hypocrisy they match their sceptical honesty: politely but persistently; with formality and also with futility.

Her characters include children, treated with sensitivity and understanding, servants whose language derives from a Dickensian delight in departure from the norm, and those whose infirmities divert the discriminating reader. Their conversations carry on the action of a novel with a calmness which is deceptive: in the process we come to realise the evil innate in these men and women, for the plots revealed by these controlled conversations are often highly melodramatic.

It is necessary to read Miss Compton-Burnett with intelligence, paying attention to her moral insight. For her scheme of things affords no poetic justice: there are, she says, two worlds and their ways; there are parents and children; there is the present and the past; and there is darkness and day. Upon sinister darkness Miss Compton-Burnett throws the light of day; her wit illuminates our age through the lens of tradition; but she has found new, economical ways of grinding that lens, she affords a high degree of magnification of the human situation which she explores so discreetly yet devastatingly. She can do all this because of the distinction with which she handles language; she speaks out of deep seriousness and wisdom and presents her superbly comic and her profoundly tragic situations with originality and a rare artistic integrity.

Your Royal Highness and Chancellor, I present to you IVY COMPTON-BURNETT for the degree of Doctor of Letters, *honoris causa*.

II

THE SPOKEN WORD

I. Compton-Burnett and M. Jourdain

A CONVERSATION

M. J.   We are both what our country landladies call 'great readers', and have often talked over other people's books during this long quarter of a century between two wars, but never *your* books.

I. C.-B.   It seems an omission, as I am sure we have talked of yours. So let us remedy it.

M. J.   I see that yours are a novel thing in fiction, and unlike the work of other novelists. I see that they are conversation pieces, stepping into the bounds of drama, that narrative and exposition in them are drastically reduced, that there is less scenery than in the early days of the English drama, when a placard informed the audience that the scene was 'a wood near Athens', and less description than in many stage directions. There is nothing to catch the eye, in this 'country of the blind'. All your books, from *Pastors and Masters*, to the present-day *Elders and Betters* are quite unlike what Virginia Woolf called the 'heavy upholstered novel'.

I. C.-B.   I do not see why exposition and description are a necessary part of a novel. They are not of a play, and both deal with imaginary human beings and their lives. I have been told that I ought to write plays, but cannot see myself making the transition. I read plays with especial pleasure, and in reading novels I am disappointed if a scene is carried through in the voice of the author rather than the voices of the characters. I think that I simply follow my natural bent. But I hardly think that 'country of the blind' is quite the right description of my scene.

M. J.   I should like to ask you one or two questions; partly my own and partly what several friends have asked. There is time enough and to spare in Lyme Regis, which is a town well-known to novelists. Jane Austen was here, and Miss Mitford.

I. C.-B.   And now we are here, though our presence does not seem to be equally felt. No notice marks our lodging. And we also differ from Jane Austen and Miss Mitford in being birds of passage, fleeing from bombs. I have a feeling that they would both have fled, and felt it proper to do so, and wish that we could really feel it equally proper.

M. J.   I have heard your dialogue criticised as 'highly artificial' or stylised. One reviewer, I remember, said that it was impossible to 'conceive of any human being giving tongue to every emotion, foible and reason with the precision, clarity and wit possessed by all Miss Compton-Burnett's characters, be they parlourmaids, children, parents or spinster aunts'. It seems odd to object to precision, clarity and wit, and the same objection would lie against the dialogue of Congreve and Sheridan.

I. C.-B.   I think that my writing does not seem to me as 'stylised' as it apparently is, though I do not attempt to make my characters use the words of actual life. I cannot tell you why I write as I do, as I do not know. I have even tried not to do it, but find myself falling back into my own way. It seems to me that the servants in my books talk quite differently from the educated people, and the children from the adults, but the difference may remain in my own mind and not be conveyed to the reader. I think people's style, like the way they speak and move, comes from themselves and cannot be explained. I am not saying that they necessarily admire it, though naturally they turn on it a lenient eye.

M. J.   The word 'stylised', which according to the *New English Dictionary* means 'conforming to the rules of a conventional style' has been used in reviewing your books, but the dialogue is often very close to real speech, and not 'artificial' or 'stylised'. It is, however, sometimes interrupted by formal speech. Take Lucia Sullivan's explanation of her grandfather's reluctance to enter his son's sitting-room without an invitation. 'It is the intangibility of the distinction (she says) that gives it its point'. Lucia Sullivan is a girl of twenty-four, not especially formal at other times.

I. C.-B.   I cannot tell why my people talk sometimes according to conventional style, and sometimes in the manner of real speech, if this is the case. It is simply the result of an effort to give the impression I want to give.

I should not have thought that Lucia Sullivan's speech was particularly formal. The long word near the beginning is the word that gives her meaning; and surely a girl of twenty-four is enough of a woman to have a normal command of words.

M. J.   Reviewers lean to comparisons. Some have suggested a likeness between your work and Jane Austen's. Mr Edwin Muir, however, thinks it is 'much nearer the Elizabethan drama of horror'—I can't think why.

I. C.-B.   I should not have thought that authors often recognised influences. They tend to think, and to like to think, that they are not unduly indebted to their predecessors. But I have read Jane Austen so much, and with such enjoyment and admiration, that I may have absorbed things from her unconsciously. I do not think myself that my books have any real likeness to hers. I think that there is possibly some likeness between our minds.

The same might apply in a measure to the Elizabethan dramatists, though I don't think I have read these more than most people have.

M. J.   Mr Muir in an earlier review says that you remind him of Congreve—a formidable list, Congreve, Jane Austen, Henry James and the Elizabethan dramatists—and the odd thing is that they are all disparate.

I. C.-B.   The only explanation I can give, is that people who practise the same art are likely to have some characteristics in common. I have noticed such resemblance between writers the most widely separated, in merit, kind and time.

M. J.   I see one point of contact between your novels and Jane Austen's. She keeps her eye fixed upon the small circle of country gentlefolk who seem to have little to do but pay calls, take walks, talk, and dine, in fact—the comfortable classes; she does not include people in what Austen Leigh calls 'a position of poverty and obscurity, as this, though not necessarily connected with vulgarity, has a sad tendency to degenerate into it.'

I. C.-B.   I feel that I do not know the people outside my own world well enough to deal with them. I had no idea that my characters did nothing but call, walk, talk and dine, though I am glad you do not say that they only talk. Their professions and occupations are indicated, but I am concerned with their personal lives; and following them into their professional world would lead to the alternations between two spheres, that I think is a mistake in books. I always regret it in the great Victorian novelists, though it would be hard to avoid it in books on a large scale. And my characters have their own poverty and obscurity, though of course it is only their own.

I feel I have a knowledge of servants in so far as they take a part in the world they serve. This may mean that the knowledge is superficial, as I have often thought it in other people's books.

The people in between seem to me unrelated to anything I know. When I talk to tradespeople, their thoughts and reactions seem to have their background in a dark world, though their material lives may not differ greatly from my own.

M. J. I don't see any influence of the 'Elizabethan drama of horror', nor much of Jane Austen. I think there is something of Henry James. What about the suggestion that the Russian novelists affected you—not Tolstoy of course, but Chekhov or Dostoevsky. Dostoevsky's method, 'a mad jumble that flings things down in a heap', isn't yours. And how about the Greek dramatists?

I. C.-B. I am not a great reader of Henry James, though I have seen it suggested that I am his disciple. I don't mean that I have any objection to the character, except in so far as it is a human instinct to object to being a disciple, but I hardly think I have read him enough to show his influence. I enjoy him less than many other writers. He does not reveal as much as I should like of the relations of his characters with each other. And I am surprised if my style is as intricate as his. I should have thought it was only rather condensed. If it is, I sympathise with the people who cannot read my books. The Russian novels I read with a sense of being in a daze, of seeing their action take place in a sort of half-light, as though there was an obscurity between my mind and theirs, and only part of the meaning conveyed to a Russian came through to me. I always wonder if people, who think they see the whole meaning, have any conception of it. So I am probably hardly influenced by the Russians. But, as I have said before, I think that people who follow the same art, however different their levels, are likely to have some of the same attributes, and that it is possibly these that lead them to a similar end. The Greek dramatists I read as a girl, as I was classically educated, and read them with the attention to each line necessitated by the state of my scholarship; and it is difficult to say how much soaked in, but I should think very likely something. I have not read them for many years— another result of the state of my scholarship.

M. J. There is little attention given to external things and almost no descriptive writing in your novels, and that is a breach with tradition. Even Jane Austen has an aside about the 'worth' of Lyme, Charmouth and Pinhay, 'with its green chasms between romantic rocks'. And there is much more description in later novels, such as Thomas Hardy's. In 'The Return of the Native', the great Egdon Heath has to be reckoned with as a protagonist. Now you cut out all this. The Gavestons' house in *A Family and a Fortune* is spoken of as old and beautiful, but its date and style are not mentioned.

I. C.-B. I should have thought that my actual characters were described enough to help people to imagine them. However detailed such description is, I am sure that everyone forms his own conceptions, that are different from everyone else's, including the author's. As regards such things as landscape and scenery, I never feel inclined to describe them; indeed I tend to miss such writing out, when I am reading, which may be a sign that I am not fitted for it. I make an exception of Thomas Hardy, but surely his presentation of natural features almost as characters puts him on a plane of his own, and almost carries the thing described into the human world. In the case of Jane Austen, I hurry through her words about Lyme and its surroundings, in order to return to her people.

It might be better to give more account of people's homes and intimate background, but I hardly see why the date and style of the Gavestons' house should be given, as I did not think of them as giving their attention to it, and as a house of a different date and style would have done for them equally well. It would be something to them that it was old and beautiful, but it would be enough.

M. J. I see a reviewer says that *Elders and Betters*—which has the destruction of a will by one character (Anna Donne) who afterwards drives another to suicide—has 'a milder and less criminal flavour than most of its predecessors'. There is a high incidence of murder in some of your novels, which is really not common among the 'comfortable classes'. I remember, however, talking of the rarity of murders with a lawyer's daughter, who said that her father asserted that murders within their class were not so rare. He used to call them 'Mayfair murders'.

I. C.-B.　I never see why murder and perversion of justice are not normal subjects for a plot, or why they are particularly Elizabethan or Victorian, as some reviewers seem to think. But I think it is better for a novel to have a plot. Otherwise it has no shape, and incidents that have no part in a formal whole seem to have less significance. I always wish that Katherine Mansfield's *At the Bay* was cast in a formal mould. And a plot gives rise to secondary scenes, that bring out personality and give scope for revealing character. If the plot were taken out of a book, a good deal of what may seem unconnected with it, would have to go. A plot is like the bones of a person, not interesting like expression or signs of experience, but the support of the whole.

M. J.　*At the Bay* breaks off rather than comes to its full stop. A novel without a plot sags like a tent with a broken pole. Your last book had a very generous amount of review space; and most of the reviews were intelligent. Elizabeth Bowen found a phrase for one of your characteristics; 'a sinister cosiness', but the *Queen* tells one that 'if one perseveres with the conversations' (evidently an obstacle) 'a domestic chronicle of the quieter sort emerges'. How do you think reviews have affected you and your work?

I. C.-B.　It is said that writers never read reviews, but in this case it is hard to see how the press-cutting agencies can flourish and increase their charge. I think that writers not only read reviews, but are subject to an urge to do so. George Henry Lewes is supposed to have hidden George Eliot's disparaging reviews, in case she should see them; and if he wished to prevent her doing so, I think it was a wise precaution. I think that reviews have a considerable effect upon writers. Of course I am talking of reviews that count, by people whose words have a meaning. I remember my first encouraging notices with gratitude to their authors. Much of the pleasure of making a book would go, if it held nothing to be shared by other people. I would write for a few dozen people; and it sometimes seems that I do so; but I would not write for no one.

I think the effect of reviews upon a writer's actual work is less. A writer is too happy in praise to do anything but accept it. Blame he would reject, if he could; but if he cannot, I think he generally knew of his guilt, and could not remedy matters. I have nearly always found this the case myself.

Letters from readers must come under the head of reviews, and have the advantage that their writers are under no compulsion to mention what they do not admire. I have only had one correspondent who broke this rule, and what he did not admire was the whole book. He stated that he could see nothing in it, and had moreover found it too concentrated to read. Someone said that I must have liked this letter the most of all I had had, but I believe I liked it the least.

Some writers have so many letters that they find them a burden. They make me feel ashamed of having so few, and inclined to think that people should write to me more.

M. J.   In all your work you go back to the period between the South African war and the 'Great' war, when time stood still. One novel (*A Family and a Fortune*) is dated 1901, and the others are all round the same date. England is still on the gold standard; the miser Clement Gaveston has a pile of sovereigns in his desk—carriages are horse-drawn, and there is an ample supply of servants.

I. C.-B.   I do not feel that I have any real or organic knowledge of life later than about 1910. I should not write of later times with enough grasp or confidence. I think this is why many writers tend to write of the past. When an age is ended, you see it as it is. And I have a dislike, which I cannot explain, of dealing with modern machinery and inventions. When war casts its shadow, I find that I recoil.

M. J.   Did you take any suggestions for the characters or plots in your novels from actual life; I mean from our own friends and acquaintances?

I. C.-B.   I think that actual life supplies a writer with characters much less than is thought. Of course there must be a beginning to every conception, but so much change seems to take place in it at once, that almost anything comes to serve the purpose—a face of a stranger, a face in a portrait, almost a face in the fire. And people in life hardly seem to be definite enough to appear in print. They are not good or bad enough, or clever or stupid enough, or comic or pitiful enough. They would have to be presented by means of detailed description, and would not come through in talk. I think that the reason why a person is often angered by a supposed portrait of himself, is that the author leaves in some recognisable attributes, while the conception has altered so much that the subject is justified in thinking there is no resemblance. And I believe that we know much less of each other than we think, that it would be a great shock to find oneself suddenly behind another person's eyes. The things we think we know about each other, we may often imagine and read in. I think this is another reason why a supposed portrait gives offence. It is really far from the truth.

In cases where a supposed portrait of some living person has caused trouble, I have thought that the explanation lies in these things, and that the author's disclaimer of any intention of portraiture is in the main sincere and just.

As regards plots I find real life no help at all. Real life seems to have no plots. And as I think a plot desirable and almost necessary, I have this extra grudge against life. But I think there are signs that strange things happen, though they do not emerge. I believe it would go ill with many of us, if we were faced by a strong temptation, and I suspect that with some of us it does go ill.

M. J.   Several writers are at their best in the mood of recollection—Thomas Hardy for instance. The immediate past also gives more complete specimens of the fabric of parental authority.

Sir Jesse Sullivan in *Parents and Children* 'believes in his divine right', and his son accepts his position. Isolation and leisure seem necessary for the rearing of strange family growths.

I. C.-B.   Isolation and leisure put nothing into people. But they give what is there, full play. They allow it to grow according to itself, and this may be strongly in certain directions.

I am sure that the people who were middle-aged and elderly when I was young, were more individualised than are now my own contemporaries. The effect of wider intercourse and self-adaptation seems to go below the surface, and the result is that the essence of people is controlled and modified. The people may be better and do less harm, but they afford less interest as a study. This is surely the real meaning of the saying that personalities belong to the past.

Imagine a Winston Churchill, untaught and untrained and un-adapted in the sense we mean, and then immured in an isolated life in a narrow community, and think what might have happened to his power, what would have happened to it.

The assumption of divine right and the acceptance of it takes things further along the same line. History gives us examples, that are repeated in smaller kingdoms.

M. J.   I don't think you have the note-book habit. I mean the collection of unrelated notes of things seen and heard. Katherine Mansfield filled note-books with memoranda and worked these up into what she called vignettes, or into her stories. She also made notes of phrases and sentences for as she said, 'one never knows when a little tag like that may come in useful to round off a paragraph.' I like to know how people work.

I. C.-B.   I dare say you do, but the people themselves are not always quite sure. I have not the note-book habit; that is, I do not watch or listen to strangers with a view to using the results. They do not do or say things that are of any good. They are too in-definite and too much alike and are seldom living in anything but the surface of their lives. Think how rarely we should ourselves say or do anything that would throw light on our characters or experience.

But as I have already said, some sort of starting-point is useful; and I get it almost anywhere; and I doubt if Katherine Mansfield really got more help than this from what she saw and heard. You say she worked it up, and I am sure she must have done so.

I cannot understand her noting phrases and sentences for future use, and find it hard to believe that they served any purpose. Rounding off a paragraph, occurring in the normal course of writing, by a tag overheard and stored up, seems to me too unnatural to be possible. She said that she never knew when such things would come in useful, and I suspect that she never found out.

M. J.   What is odd, but of course it isn't serious criticism, is the recoil of some reviewers from what they call 'the sorry spectacle of adult human nature' presented in your novels, as if they were a board examining the degrees of moral turpitude among a group of immigrants. Yours are not the *only* doubtful characters in fiction! And when characters are accepted, even the *New States-man* 'violently hoped for a quite different, a more vindictive ending of *Elders and Betters*'. Is it the old demand for what was called 'poetic justice', the calling in the world of fiction to redress the balance of the real world?

I. C.–B. I should have said that there were a good many good people in my books, and this may mean that I hardly see eye-to-eye with the reviewers. But I think that life makes great demand on people's characters, and gives them, and especially used to give them, great opportunity to serve their own ends by the sacrifice of other people. Such ill-doing may meet with little retribution, may indeed be hardly recognised, and I cannot feel so surprised if people yield to it.

I have been told that I treat evil-doing as if it were normal, and am not normally repelled by it, and this may be putting my own words in another form. As you say, there are many doubtful characters in other fiction. Something must happen in a novel, and wrong-doing makes a more definite picture or event. Virtue tends to be more even and less spectacular, and it does not command so much more sympathy, as is proved by the accepted tendency of the villain to usurp the hero's place.

The *New Statesman* wanted wickedness to be punished, but my point is that it is not punished, and that that is why it is natural to be guilty of it. When it is likely to be punished, most of us avoid it. I do not think this desire is the old demand for poetic justice, any more than the normal demand for actual justice. In a book there hardly seems to be any difference.

M. J. Going back to the reviews I have just quoted, it is only *adult* human nature that is criticised. This reminds me that in *Parents and Children* children play as large a part as parents. Is that not a change?

I. C.–B. Yes, it is a change, though one or two children have appeared in my other books. I think it may be the result of an instinct to do something different.

It is difficult to avoid apparent repetition, if books remain too much on the same line. The words, 'apparent repetition', are my own, and it may in effect be real repetition. However differently characters are conceived—and I have never conceived two in the same way—they tend to give a similar impression, if they are people of the same kind, produced by the same mind, and carried out by the same hand, and possibly one that is acquiring a habit.

And I do not think children have less interest than older people. I think their experience tends to be deeper and sharper, and even if more transitory—and I am not sure of this after very early years —to leave a deeper impression and memory. This seems to be borne out by the current phrases about the despair and ecstasy and observation of childhood.

But I do not claim that the children in my books, any more than their elders, resemble the actual creatures of real life. When I meet them, they are open to the same objection, and fail to afford me assistance.

And now I feel I know nothing more about myself, and hope the inquisition is at an end. And in spite of what I said about Katherine Mansfield, I am sorry that I have no tag stored up to round off the last paragraph.

Orion I, 1945

Michael Millgate

INTERVIEW WITH MISS COMPTON-BURNETT

SCENE: Miss Compton-Burnett's flat on the first floor of a heavy, 'Scottish-baronial' mansion in a quiet Kensington backwater just off Cromwell Road. The room is large, with a lofty ceiling, tall, broad windows, and walls that are a cold expanse of green relieved by several hanging mirrors, but by only one small picture. Along the walls are ranged several pieces of fine eighteenth-century furniture but the centre of the room is quite bare. The desk at which Miss Compton-Burnett writes is placed between the windows and the fire, but it was at the fire itself, on that November afternoon, that we sat, talked, and recorded the interview.

Miss Compton-Burnett wore a long, black dress, and her grey hair was bound tightly with a band. Her face is strong, with a suggestion of severity that contrasts greatly with her manner, which is disarmingly kind, eager and alert. In the book-case were leather-bound editions of 'the classics'—Shakespeare, Jane Austen, Dr Johnson, Addison, Fielding, Bunyan—but the conversation over tea was mainly about recent books and plays. We talked about *Look Back in Anger*, Sir Charles Snow's Rede Lecture, and Joyce Cary. Miss Compton-Burnett was just about to read John Braine's new novel. Later she spoke of her family, of the First World War, of the insularity of British intellectuals, which she deplored while confessing that she shared it, and of a recent encounter with Mr T. S. Eliot ('We seemed to talk about food all the time'). In conversation, as in the interview itself, she spoke swiftly, surely, without hesitation and, apparently, with enjoyment.

INTERVIEWER   Had you written much before *Dolores*?

I. C.-B.   No, hardly at all: only just childish things that everybody writes who is probably going to be a writer, nothing that I wanted to publish or that I wish I had published.

INTERVIEWER   It was your first completed novel?

I. C.-B.   Yes.

INTERVIEWER   Could you explain the long gap between *Dolores* and *Pastors and Masters*?

I. C.-B.   There were reasons in my own life. Family troubles and responsibilities and the loss of a brother in the war. And a bad illness took all my energy away for some years, and I thought the best thing was to let it come back by itself, and in the end it did. I expect that is why I can go on writing so late.

INTERVIEWER   Did you always want to write?

I. C.-B.   I think I always felt I should, and I think my brothers did too. You remember I told you I lost two brothers: one, who was a Fellow of King's at Cambridge, was killed in the Somme battles in 1916, and he would have been a writer I'm sure—and the elder one too. I think we always assumed that we should write, and talked as if we should. Our parents were interested in writing, and we grew up with the feeling.

INTERVIEWER   Do you now write every day?

I. C.-B.   No, I write at my own times. I generally wait about a year after one book before I begin another, and then I think I must write fairly quickly, as people go, to get it done in a year. So it amounts to writing slowly because of the gaps.

INTERVIEWER   But when you are actually working on a novel you write it in about a year?

I. C.-B.   I seem to—yes, I think so.

INTERVIEWER   If you are working, about how many words would you write in a day?

I. C.-B.   Quite a few words, if they are going to stand.

INTERVIEWER   Do you revise a great deal? Do you make corrections or redraft?

I. C.-B.   No, I don't think I revise a great deal. I make full notes, almost like a first draft, and then make another. Corrections I make quite freely: I haven't anything against making them. Of course, I don't know how many other people make.

INTERVIEWER   But there would only be the one draft in effect?

I. C.-B.   Yes, only the one real draft, but the first notes are so full so that it is almost like a second.

INTERVIEWER   Do you need or prefer any particular conditions to work in?

B

I. C.-B.   Quiet and not too much interruption. I always get a certain amount of the last.

INTERVIEWER   Do you ever read your work aloud at any stage?

I. C.-B.   Not actually aloud, but, as anyone must, I think, who writes in dialogue, I seem to hear the words said.

INTERVIEWER   Do you ever rehearse them to yourself?

I. C.-B.   No, I don't do that.

INTERVIEWER   In the *Orion* interview you said that you did not have the notebook habit in the Katherine Mansfield way.

I. C.-B.   No, I don't, and I can never understand how anyone can. I find it very hard to believe that she had it as much as she says. I simply don't understand how she could listen in different places and hear dialogue that she could use. People always seem to me to talk so flatly. I only hear casual sentences that throw no light on anything.

INTERVIEWER   What do you do when you get an idea for a plot or a situation or anything like that? Don't you jot it down anywhere?

I. C.-B.   I don't jot it down, but I keep it in my head. I don't forget it if I have it; so it comes to the same thing. I suppose people are afraid that they will forget it, but I don't think they would. If you had an idea, you would find it too valuable to forget.

INTERVIEWER   You don't have a set of plans for future novels?

I. C.-B.   No, I don't. Joyce Cary came to tea with me once and said to me, 'Don't you find it awkward when you have the material for fifteen novels in your head, and you don't know how to cope with them all at once?' I have never had the material for more than one at a time. As I write one, something might occur to me for the next, but it is never more than that.

INTERVIEWER   Is it possible for you to describe how the individual novel takes shape?

I. C.-B.   No, I don't think it is. It seems to take shape by itself, which I suppose is a way of saying that I form it subconsciously.

INTERVIEWER   Do you think about it for a long time before you begin writing?

I. C.-B.   I think I must plan it subconsciously, because after about a year it seems to be trying to come out. I think people work at very different levels of consciousness: I think I must work rather low down. I don't think it makes any difference in the end.

INTERVIEWER Do all your novels come out in the same way?

I. C.-B. More or less. Yes, I think so, as far as anything is ever the same as anything else.

INTERVIEWER But when you actually come to write, you come to it with a sense of assurance: you have a fair idea of what you are going to do?

I. C.-B. Well, if I can get the thing completely mapped out in my head, I go to it with more assurance than if I just start with something and hope it will develop of itself. In the end it does, but in that case you lose assurance.

INTERVIEWER You don't often make a false start?

I. C.-B. No, I don't think I do that, but when I have got a good long way in a book, I have to go back sometimes and modify the beginning, because sometimes the book alters, though I find not so very much.

INTERVIEWER Could we come on to the question of your plots, which people are often puzzled and sometimes appalled by. Do you have any particular source for these?

I. C.-B. No, I don't know how I get them. I think something must happen in a book—or there is no book. It seems to me that a book must have a structure. It may be an old-fashioned view, but I am surprised by some of these modern books which have no structure at all, but are just a piece of life carved out. It isn't natural for me to write like that. I seem to want a bone foundation for them. The structure is in a sense the bone of the book.

INTERVIEWER Critics have sometimes seen suggestions in your novels of the themes of Greek drama. Are you conscious of any such influence?

I. C.-B. I'm not conscious of it but I was classically educated both as a child and at college, and it would not be unnatural if something had come through.

INTERVIEWER I wonder if I could mention just briefly one or two of the other people to whom you have been compared: what about Jane Austen and Henry James?

I. C.-B. I have a great admiration for Jane Austen and I know her books well. Henry James I have read very little, although people have said I'm his disciple. I can't possibly be that, as I haven't read him enough. To be honest, I find him difficult to read on the whole.

INTERVIEWER   What about George Eliot?

I. C.-B.   I like her books very much—the fresh and lively part of them—not the instructive or moralising part. I like the first part of *Adam Bede* and *The Mill on the Floss*; and of course I like *Middlemarch*.

INTERVIEWER Yes, there does seem to be a strong influence of George Eliot in *Dolores*, if I might say so.

I. C.-B.   Yes, well, there may be, because I read a good deal of her then. I haven't read her nearly so much for a good many years.

INTERVIEWER   Are you aware of any other direct literary influences on your work?

I. C.-B.   No, I don't think I am. But I think that people who do the same work naturally have some of the same qualities. When I hear people say that someone is indebted to somebody else, I often think he may not even have read him. It may be that people who are in the same line have the attributes that led them to it. I suppose two cooks would have a light hand, and two tailors a good cut. I think that must be the same with all kinds of work.

INTERVIEWER   Yes, except that a cook has to learn from another cook and a tailor must serve his apprenticeship.

I. C.-B.   Yes, but even a writer has to learn his own language. As I say, I think that people are often supposed to be influenced by someone, when it is simply that they have similar gifts. They must have them to get along the same road.

INTERVIEWER   Your dialogue has been compared with that of dramatists like Congreve and Oscar Wilde. Quite apart from this question of likeness and influence, it is impossible not to wonder about the source of the theatrical quality in your novels, which comes out particularly well when they are broadcast.

I. C.-B.   I haven't read either Congreve or Oscar Wilde more than most people read them. Of course, I have read Oscar Wilde's plays and seen and enjoyed them, and I remember enjoying Congreve's *Love for Love*. But I haven't read either enough to be influenced by him.

INTERVIEWER But you did have, and I think you still have, a particular interest in the theatre?

I. C.-B. I'm very fond of the theatre, and I like reading plays very much. I have a great admiration for Chekhov's plays. When I'm at the theatre I like seeing into a dramatist's mind as well as watching what happens on the stage.

INTERVIEWER You always have gone to the theatre a great deal?

I. C.-B. Well, I have gone regularly.

INTERVIEWER But you have never actually tried to write a play?

I. C.-B. No, I never have. I think a novel gives you more scope. I think I should call my books something between a novel and a play, and I feel the form suits me better than the pure play. It gives me more range and a little more length, and it doesn't subject me to the mechanical restrictions of a play.

INTERVIEWER In *Pastors and Masters* you already have the conception of the dialogue novel. Do you recall how the idea came to you?

I. C.-B. No, I have no idea. I suppose it was just natural to me.

INTERVIEWER You have never tried to write a different kind of book?

I. C.-B. No, I never have.

INTERVIEWER And you have had no ambition to do so?

I. C.-B. No.

INTERVIEWER Are there any special novelists you admire and would like to emulate?

I. C.-B. I've never felt that I would like to emulate anyone. As I've said before, I don't think that people do feel that. I think they feel that they would like to improve their own work along their own lines, but that is a different thing.

INTERVIEWER Are there any particular directions in which you feel you would like to improve yours?

I. C.-B. Well, I sometimes think I'd like the books to be a little longer and fuller, but I hate padding. I like condensed work, but that may be because it is natural for me to write condensed.

INTERVIEWER You once said that you didn't feel at ease with

life after about 1910. Does this feeling extend to the art and literature produced since then?

I. C.-B.   No, I don't think it does. I think that is rather different. But I should find it difficult to write of things when they are in a state of flux. I find it natural to write of them when they are, in a way, finished, as do many of the writers of the past. It's better to take great writers, because everybody knows them—people like Dickens and Thackeray and George Eliot. They waited until a part of life was complete and they could look back and see it as a whole.

INTERVIEWER   Jane Austen didn't of course, but . . .

I. C.-B.   No, that is true. But there wasn't really much flux, was there, in her time?

INTERVIEWER   You say the feeling doesn't extend to literature since 1910: I wonder if there are any modern authors you read and particularly admire?

I. C.-B.   Well, there are many authors I enjoy reading. Elizabeth Bowen, Graham Greene, L. P. Hartley and Arnold Bennett in parts. I think Bennett is underestimated. I think his 'Five Towns' work is better than it is supposed to be.

INTERVIEWER   He's becoming more respectable, isn't he?

I. C.-B.   I think so. I wish he hadn't written a lot of blown up books like the *Grand Babylon Hotel*, but I like parts of *The Old Wives' Tale* and parts of *Clayhanger* and a good deal of *Anna of the Five Towns*. And I like the books that are a kind of joke like *The Great Man* and *The Card*. I don't think it's great writing, but I think he is more talented than he has been supposed to be, and I'd also call him a good critic. Another book I like is Hugh Walpole's *The Old Ladies*. If he had given more time to it (he wrote it in six weeks I believe), it might have grown to something much better than the general run of his work.

INTERVIEWER   What about Forster?

I. C.-B.   Well, you know, if I am to be quite honest, I think he's overestimated. I don't say that I don't think he is a man of high talent. I think he is, but not a genius. What do you think?

INTERVIEWER   I have a great admiration for him, but this is partly due to my feeling for him as a liberal thinker, as a political figure.

I. C.-B.   Yes, there is that of course, and don't think I don't admire his books. I do admire them and *Howards End* I know very well. I am an insular person and enjoy that more than *A Passage to India*. I think he is a very good writer, but not a great one.

INTERVIEWER   What about Virginia Woolf?

I. C.-B.   Well, is she really a novelist?

INTERVIEWER   It's an open question, perhaps.

I. C.-B.   I admire her use of words, I enjoy most of her work, but I wouldn't actually call her a good novelist.

INTERVIEWER   There's a lack of bone?

I. C.-B.   A lack of bone and a lack of character drawing, I think. I think her work is different.

INTERVIEWER   You've not felt yourself strongly influenced by any of the modern experimental novelists?

I. C.-B.   No.

INTERVIEWER   Are there any other writers, not necessarily novelists, for whom you have an admiration or affection? What about the eighteenth-century writers like Pope?

I. C.-B.   I do enjoy Pope very much. I think Defoe's *Robinson Crusoe* is a very good book, and also Fielding's *Tom Jones*. But I think they are the only great books that the authors wrote.

INTERVIEWER   I was really leading up in a roundabout way to the question of whether there is any relationship between your literary likes and dislikes, and the names you give to some of your characters.

I. C.-B.   No, not really. Of course, I was conscious that they were the names of writers.

INTERVIEWER   You say in the *Orion* interview that you have never conceived two characters in the same way.

I. C.-B.   I've never conceived two characters in the same way. I think sometimes some of my characters have turned out more alike than I meant them to be, and too like people in my other books. I think sometimes one doesn't get all one's meaning through.

INTERVIEWER   Is it possible for you to say anything about how you do in fact conceive them?

I. C.-B.   I don't think so. I don't think anyone could do that. I don't think you ever know how you do a thing. If you write a postcard, you don't know how you do it.

INTERVIEWER   You have no idea how the idea of a character actually comes to you, and where it starts from?

I. C.-B.   No, it just does come.

INTERVIEWER   Do you have a visual impression?

I. C.-B.   Well, I see my characters. I feel as if I'm looking at them.

INTERVIEWER   Is that part of the original conception, or does it come later?

I. C.-B.   It's part of the original conception, but I think it grows sometimes, as I go on looking at the characters.

INTERVIEWER   To your knowledge, you have never actually drawn upon people?

I. C.-B.   No, not really. A person is a jumping off ground at the most. A character may come from a picture or a strange face. A woman may become a man, or an old man a girl. That sort of thing does happen.

INTERVIEWER   It has been suggested that some of the people in your novels are almost 'humour' characters or personified virtues and vices. Has this been part of your intention?

I. C.-B.   Not part of my intention, but I can't say that it isn't the case. It's so difficult to know whether you have got everything that was in your mind, through. I've never conceived a character in that way or wanted one to be like that, but if some of them seem so, perhaps I have made them so in spite of myself.

INTERVIEWER   It is sometimes said that your conception of characters is rather static—the characters spring fully armed into the opening pages of the novel, and are more or less unchanged at the end. We simply know them better.

I. C.-B.   Yes, I think that is true. The action of my books, on the whole, covers a short time, so that it is hardly possible for a character to grow. It takes a long time for a human being to change.

INTERVIEWER   I notice in *A Heritage and Its History*—you showed development there.

I. C.-B.   Yes, because there was more time.

INTERVIEWER   Do you feel affection for your characters?

I. C.-B.   Yes, I feel affection for nearly all of them—for the bad as well as the good.

INTERVIEWER   Are there any that you particularly cherish?

I. C.-B.   No, I think I cherish them equally. We all know dubious characters whom we would hardly have altered. Of course, some of the minor ones I don't cherish as much as the main ones.

INTERVIEWER   Do you think much about the book when you have finished it? Do you like to re-read it?

I. C.-B.   No, when I re-read them I find that they drag me back into themselves, and that after the first few pages it is difficult to read them as if I were reading them for the first time. I should think that most writers find that.

INTERVIEWER   In your more recent novels the race of monsters, like Josephine Napier and Matilda Seaton and so on, seems to have died out. Is there any particular reason for that?

I. C.-B.   No, it was just that I had finished with them and went on to something else. They don't seem to me such monsters as they do to other people. I think, as I have said many times, that a good many of us, if subjected to a strong and sudden temptation, without any risk of being found out, would yield to it. That is my own opinion.

INTERVIEWER   Have you ever changed the matter or manner of your novels in response to criticism?

I. C.-B.   No, I haven't. I suppose you are taking adverse criticism. You either agree with it or you don't. If you agree, I think you probably have tried to correct the fault and can't, and if you don't agree, you can only think the critic is wrong.

INTERVIEWER   But you do read reviews of your books?

I. C.-B.   Yes, I subscribe to a press cutting agency, and they come to me.

INTERVIEWER   Do you write with a particular audience in mind?

I. C.-B.   I didn't at first. But as I've gone on writing, I have found myself writing for what people call 'their public'—a misleading term for a limited number of readers like mine. I think there is a feeling that you want to please the people who read and enjoy your books.

INTERVIEWER   And you have a fairly clear conception of what they want?

I. C.-B.   I think it is more a question of what one can do, and they have to accept. The people who like it and want it are those who make your public.

INTERVIEWER   Do you think you make unusual demands upon them?

I. C.-B.   No, not if they are intelligent people who will read a book word for word. I do think my books need that. It does not seem to me an unreasonable demand. If someone reads every other page or a sentence here and there, he writes the kind of criticism that shows that the book has eluded him, or rather that he has eluded the book. I think my books are rather condensed, but I don't think they are obscure.

INTERVIEWER   How do you respond to the feeling of some critics that you have steadily progressed as a novelist, constantly extending the scope and richness of your work?

I. C.-B.   I don't think I should have thought I had progressed much, on the whole.

INTERVIEWER   Do you feel that you have achieved more success with one particular book than you have with others?

I. C.-B.   Well, favourites of mine are *Manservant and Maidservant* and the first two-thirds of *A House and Its Head*. But I don't think there is a great difference in the quality of the books; and I think this is borne out by the fact that people who write to me saying which is their favourite, choose such different ones.

INTERVIEWER   Do you get many letters?

I. C.-B.   No. As far as I can gather from what other writers say, I have very few. I have some nice, serious ones that I answer myself. I don't have the number that some people apparently have. Elizabeth Bowen told me that when she wrote *The Death of the Heart*, she had thousands of letters. Not so much about her book as about the writers' similar experiences.

INTERVIEWER   Perhaps if we had had experiences like those in your books we would keep quiet about them.

I. C.-B.   Well, perhaps that is so—perhaps that is what it is.

INTERVIEWER   Which of your books did you particularly enjoy writing, do you remember?

I. C.-B.   I think *Manservant and Maidservant*, but not in any strong sense.

INTERVIEWER   Because your novels don't end with the punishment of the guilty, they have been described as 'amoral'. Do you accept this description?

I. C.-B.   Not exactly. I shouldn't mind being described as amoral, but I don't think guilty people meet punishment in life. I think it is a literary convention. I think the evidence tends to show that crime on the whole pays.

INTERVIEWER   Do you think of yourself as a moralist?

I. C.-B.   Well, I don't think I've ever thought of myself as one but I believe up to a point I am. What would you say?

INTERVIEWER   There is no doubt that your good characters *are* good and your bad ones *are* bad.

I. C.-B.   Well, I should have thought there was some good in most of the bad ones. But perhaps I should not call so many of them bad.

INTERVIEWER   I wonder whether you think of your characters as being in control of their own destinies or their own personalities? Or do you feel that they are in the grip of forces greater than themselves that they are powerless to control? If so, what forces—economic, psychological, hereditary, supernatural?

I. C.-B.   I think they are all in the grip of forces—economic and psychological and hereditary. Supernatural, I shouldn't have thought myself. But I suppose that part of people's equipment is a certain power of choice and a strength of will.

INTERVIEWER   Except that they don't all have this, do they?

I. C.-B.   No, but I think many people have it in them to choose their course.

INTERVIEWER   Do you place special weight on this question of economic forces? There seem to be strong suggestions of this in some of your novels.

I. C.-B.   How do you mean?

INTERVIEWER   Well, to take the latest one, *A Heritage and Its History*, I'm thinking of the emphasis on the effect that the heritage has on Simon.

I. C.-B.   I think that economic forces influence people a great deal, that many things in their lives are bound up with them. Their scale of values, their ambitions and ideas for the future, their attitude to other people and themselves.

INTERVIEWER   Is this based entirely on observation, or have you ever read or thought about this question?

I. C.-B.   I have just accepted it. I should have thought that it would be clear to most people.

INTERVIEWER   I wonder if you have any interest in the techniques or discoveries of modern psychology?

I. C.-B.   Well, I haven't seen much of it. I should have to see more to talk of it. I haven't a great interest.

INTERVIEWER   I must say that there seems to me to be a good deal more ordinary 'niceness' in your novels than most critics have suggested. It does seem noticeable however that your good people don't *do* good.

I. C.-B.   I don't think many people have an opportunity to do good, and I sometimes think that the people who do it, like missionaries and people who do charity work, are not so very good themselves. I don't mean not virtuous, you know.

INTERVIEWER   There is a sentence in *Pastors and Masters* about what a terrible thing it must be to do good.

I. C.-B.   I think it's rather terrible to see it being done—or to have it done to oneself. On the whole I think it is rather terrible; don't you think so?

INTERVIEWER   Yes, I do. What about your 'quiet' characters, the good people living rather withdrawn from the world, like Evelyn Seymour in *Daughters and Sons*?

I. C.-B.   Well, it would be very pleasant for people to have them. They would do good in that way. In their daily relations with people they would benefit them by being as they were.

INTERVIEWER   Even though evil goes unpunished in your novels, it's not all-powerful. It may reign, in a sense, but it doesn't spread. The good and the innocent remain uncorrupted and the children, above all, seem to emerge at the end of the novel quite unharmed. I wonder if this is related to your over-all view of human nature?

I. C.-B.   Yes, I should say that it is. I think it's very difficult to alter people, very difficult either to corrupt or improve them. The essence of people remains what it is.

INTERVIEWER   This does of course temper the anguish we might otherwise feel in reading your novels.

I. C.-B. Do you mean that it is a painful spectacle to see tyranny working?

INTERVIEWER Yes.

I. C.-B. I don't think it corrupts people. I think their dislike of it, if anything, would send them the other way. I think I've seen that in life. I've seen people who were tyrannised over as children being careful not to be tyrants themselves, and people who were indulged too much as children rather tyrannical in their own families. It may be the natural reaction working.

INTERVIEWER It has been suggested that in setting your novels at around the turn of the century you were making the deliberate choice of a world free from the violence and distractions of contemporary life, a world that had already vanished but was not so far in the past as to need historical re-creation. Were you aware of making such a choice?

I. C.-B. Yes, I was aware of it. I was consciously choosing a world that was free from such violence and distractions, and therefore wasn't in a state of flux. But I don't agree that the world had vanished, or that it is vanishing now. In fact I should have thought that it had vanished less than the contemporary worlds that keep on vanishing.

INTERVIEWER I wonder if you could develop that just a little?

I. C.-B. I think that the world that I draw, that some people say has vanished, will always go on, with certain modifications that must be caused by modern life. I think that human experiences and emotions remain almost the same, and that they have more scope in that sort of set life than in the life of flux that many people lead nowadays. It seems to me that as new worlds arise and pass, the world of my books remains, and that it is getting added to, as richer people, who may come from anywhere, rise up and join it. And I think that people have always done this, and always will.

INTERVIEWER Whether it can still retain the kind of isolation that it seems to have in your novels is perhaps another question.

I. C.-B. I don't think that it had as much isolation in life as it has in my novels. I don't feel I can involve my characters much with the surroundings of people's lives. In *A House and Its Head* it has been done more than in the others. Of course people always have other people round them everywhere, but in my sort of dramatic novel, something between a novel and a play, there is hardly scope for much secondary experience.

INTERVIEWER   Has it been part of your intention to give your work a wider relevance, to make it a kind of a microcosm of the larger society?

I. C.-B.   It hasn't been my intention. I haven't even thought of it. But I think that the novels are in a way a microcosm of a larger society.

INTERVIEWER   You say somewhere that the heart of all institutions is the same . . .

I. C.-B.   Yes, in a sense it is, don't you think so?

INTERVIEWER   Yes, I think that is probably so. It has been suggested that despite the setting of your novels, the forces presented in them, particularly those that emerge as domestic tyranny, are precisely those which on a larger scale have recently produced wars and revolutions and totalitarian regimes. Have you ever thought about that?

I. C.-B.   No, I've never thought of it, but I think that the things that do produce such troubles probably are those forces. The same that produce them on a small scale in ordinary life. The sweep of them on a great scale would lead to that sort of tragedy. I think the tremendous impetus that came from Germany arose from the presence of the forces inside millions of people—not only in Hitler. Don't you think so?

INTERVIEWER   Yes. Except that Hitler was surely a very important precipitating factor?

I. C.-B.   Yes.

INTERVIEWER   Without his particular personality the movement wouldn't have taken quite that course . . .

I. C.-B.   No, probably not. It might not have taken it at all, but that would have been because people hadn't the leader to give things the specific shape. I think they would have been smouldering there just the same. In many people, you know. Of course I don't mean that there were not masses of exceptions.

INTERVIEWER   Have you begun thinking about your next novel yet?

I. C.-B.   It is, I hope, just coming.

INTERVIEWER   You have a superstition against talking about work in progress?

I. C.-B.   I don't think it's a superstition. I think it's better not to talk about it, even if you have got far enough to be able to, as I have not. You might feel that you had to keep it to the line you had described, instead of letting it grow freely. And I think that it is better for people to come to a book for the first time when it is finished.

Review of English Literature, October, 1962

I

III

THE CRITICAL WORD

Certain Reviews

Raymond Mortimer

A HOUSE AND ITS HEAD

THE COUNTRYMEN OF Henry James are now exporting a good supply of novels which have the same merits as their motor cars, speed, toughness, the ability to hold the road and a fairly good-looking shape. But how many of these products could be re-read? (And this, I take it, is a rough test of a work of art.) On the other hand, the more pretentious novels now appearing cannot, most of them, be read even once. For dazzling as are the performances of Mrs Woolf and Mr Joyce, such influence as they have had is proving disastrous, rather like that of Claude Monet in painting. Incoherence, shapelessness and a complete inability to make the figures three-dimensional are the stigmata of most 'advanced' novels: except when directed by a great stylist, the stream of consciousness ends in a mere swamp. In this country there have been one or two remarkably gifted novelists who have pursued their isolated English way unperturbed by these dangerous influences. Mr E. M. Forster, for instance, and Miss Stella Benson. But Mr Forster seems to have abandoned the novel, and Miss Stella Benson has died leaving an unfinished novel, *Mundos*, of an extraordinary excellence which aggravates one's sense of an irreparable loss. We have one novelist, however, who seems to me not only an individual of genius but a pattern of many literary virtues, Miss Compton-Burnett. At first sight her work strikes you as clumsy and heavy-fisted; her figures, though solid, are not what is called 'life-like', and she composes her books on highly defined and artificial designs. In fact, she is open to all the reproaches laid upon the founders of post-impresionism. And it is still as useless, I think, to put her work before the general public as it was to put that of Cézanne a quarter of a century ago.

Now inaccessibility is a quality which has recently acquired altogether too much prestige; among expatriate Americans in particular, the more obscure a book has been, the more extravagantly it has been praised. But the difficulty of Miss

Compton-Burnett's books comes not from obscurity but from concentration: they require very slow and attentive reading. (The best preparation for appreciating them would be, I think, an acquaintance not with *Anna Livia Plurabelle* or Miss Stein's works but with the dialogues of Plato.) She carries succinctness of expression almost to a fault, and she is ascetic in her exclusion of everything not directly to her purpose. The characters move on a stage bare of scenery and properties. They breathe, but in a vacuum. There is hardly anything but dialogue, and this is continually focused on a particular point, no incidental or introductory passages being permitted. I do not know where in literature one could find so rigorous a concentration upon the subject, except in the plays of Racine. The author encloses her characters to study their reactions rather like Pavlov inventing particular and restricted conditions for his dogs. Each chapter contains an event, described with laconic speed, which the characters then discuss in relation to themselves and to one another. Moreover, the language is stylised intensely—at first it seems grotesquely stilted, and then you perceive that it is an instrument of astounding precision. Indeed, the characters are all masters of dialectic; they pick up and play with one another's phrases like University wits of the Renaissance. Miss Compton-Burnett employs this hard and precise style on themes of extreme romantic horror, matricide and infanticide and incest. It is like hearing the plots of Aeschylus and Sophocles recounted in the cool detached tones of Miss Austen.

Miss Compton-Burnett's new novel, *A House and Its Head*, shows little change in its author. I have re-read her previous books without being able to decide which I prefer. *Brothers and Sisters* is perhaps the most amusing and *Men and Wives* the most complete, while *More Women than Men* is probably the easiest to read, at least until this new book. Her technique is steadily becoming more perfect. The method by which she tells this last story is most remarkable: we are taken straight from weddings to christenings with no indication of the passage of time. Economy could not go further. Moreover, *A House and Its Head* shows a wider range of character than any of her previous books. Though there is not a phrase in it which even a magistrate could think offensive, it is profoundly shocking, like all her books. Indeed, the 'audacity' of the works which get suppressed seems very childish and innocent by the side of her devastating and all-embracing irony.

I do not think that Miss Compton-Burnett will ever be widely popular; though her books make one laugh aloud, the demands they make upon the reader are severe. But I should like specially to recommend them to practising novelists. The novel-form has become very elastic, and it would be foolish as well as useless to wish it more rigid. But novelists could learn from this writer the enormous advantages of a classical form. Miss Compton-Burnett is not imitable, but she seems to me to sound a recall to order.

New Statesman and Nation, July 13, 1935

Elizabeth Bowen

PARENTS AND CHILDREN

'IT IS THE intangibility of the distinction that gives it its point,' says Luce, on an early page of *Parents and Children*, discussing whether her father should join her grandfather, or wait for her grandfather to join him. The residing of Fulbert, his wife Eleanor and their nine children, with Luce at the head, in the house of Fulbert's parents, Sir Jesse and Lady Sullivan, in itself creates a situation in which distinctions are bound to appear. The family fabric of pride and feeling, in which the thirteen Sullivans and their dependants all play their part, has no ordinary groundwork: it starts to rise from the level that Miss Compton-Burnett's novels, in their depiction of living, always assume. There are, that is to say, none of the obvious squalors and enmities. For instance, Lady Sullivan (Regan), of whose three children Fulbert only survives, is a furnace of motherhood, whose interior roar can be heard when some incident opens the door of her nature. But her attitude to Fulbert's wife is not hostile.

> She looked at Eleanor with a guarded, neutral expression. She could not see her with affection, as they were not bound by blood; and the motives of her son's choice of her were as obscure to her as such motives to other mothers; but she respected her for her hold on him, and was grateful to her for the children. And she had a strong appreciation of her living beneath her roof. . . . The two women lived in a formal accord, which had never come to dependence; and while each saw the other as a fellow and an equal, neither would have grieved at the other's death.

Eleanor's maternity is less positive. In fact, her lack of gift for this role is commented on by her children, constantly in her presence and unfailingly when she has left a room. Eleanor Sullivan has, at forty-eight, 'a serious, honest, somewhat equine face, and a nervous, uneasy, controlled expression'. She passes from floor to floor of the house, moves to and fro between the schoolroom and nursery, plucking upon the harp-strings of her young's sensibility with an inexpert but always hopeful hand. Throughout the early part of the book she is attempting to rally the children's feeling—attempting, in fact, to drill the nine Sullivans for climax of a sort of ballet of sorrow—for their father's forthcoming departure for South America. But Eleanor, if she does not captivate, exercises a pull of her own. She enjoys, without intermittence, Fulbert's ironic affection. And, immediately upon Fulbert's reported death, she is wooed by a neighbour, the inscrutable Ridley Cranmer.

The nine children fall into three groups—Luce, Daniel and Graham, young adults; Isabel, Venice and James, the schoolroom party, under the passive control of Miss Mitford, the governess; and Honor, Gavin and Nevill, the nursery children, under the dispensation of the nurse Hatton, her underling Mullet (of the fox-like features and the dramatized youth) and in a state of skirmish with Miss Pilbeam, the nursery governess, whose ingredients are honestness and faith. Actually, Hatton's dispensation extends a good way beyond the nursery bounds: a woman of fewer words than most of the characters, she has the Sullivan make-up perfectly taped. To say that the Sullivans have a Nannie-complex would be to speak on a lower level than the novel deserves. The relationship of the family with the two governesses is—as is usual with Miss Compton-Burnett—perfectly done: it does not cease to be analysed, from both sides, with an imperturbable lack of feeling and zest for truth. 'I like all cold; I like even ice,' says one of the children—though in another context. And an icy sharpness prevails in their dialogue. In fact, to read in these days a page of Compton-Burnett dialogue is to think of the sound of glass being swept up, one of these London mornings after a blitz. There are detonations in the Sullivan home—Fulbert's departure, his letter to Isabel, the news of his death, his widow's engagement, the show-down with Ridley, the discovery of Sir Jesse's illicit paternity—each creates a momentary shock of dullness, each is measured by this mortality of fine glass.

With each novel, Miss Compton-Burnett adds to her gallery. Figures she has already, in another novel, created, she is content—and content with deliberation—to rename and to put, in *Parents and Children*, to a this time purely formalized use. For the Cranmer family (with the exception of Faith, who is new), for the three mysterious Marlowes and for the three eldest of the nine Sullivans, Miss Compton-Burnett seems to me to rely, and rightly, on our progressive acquaintanceship with one kind of person—what one might call the illustrative rather than the functional character. In *Parents and Children*, these play subsidiary parts. In *Parents and Children* the high light falls on, and genius is evident in, the younger Sullivan children and their immediate world. Especially James and Nevill. I know no children like James and Nevill; there may be no children like James and Nevill—in fact, the point of this author's genius is that it puts out creatures to which it might defy life to approximate. James and Nevill, of a beauty divorced from sentiment, *are*, in *Parents and Children*—one cannot question them; they are more living than life. There are also Honor, Gavin, the tearful, complex, articulate Isabel, and Venice —this last more lightly, though as surely, touched in. To say that this book depicts the repercussion of grown-up crisis on children would be incorrect. The children's intensive, moment-to-moment living is for each a solitary crisis, that each maintains: grown-up sense of crisis, grown-up drama do no more than splinter upon these diamond rocks. It is the strength of Lady Sullivan, the strength of Miss Mitford, the strength of Hatton that they recognise the children's inviolability.

In this novel, as in the others, relationships remain static. The dialogue, in less than half of a phrase, in the click of a camera-shutter, shifts from place to place. The careless reader, for instance, must look back twice to discover at which point the departing Fulbert's carriage drives off. Scenes, on the other hand, are played out without mercy, to an attentuation felt by each of the characters. Most notably, the scene of Fulbert's departure. 'Well, it cannot go on much longer, boys,' Fulbert says to his elder sons, as they all stand in the hall. 'If there were any reason why it should stop,' says Graham, 'surely it would have operated by now.' Luce says: 'The train will become due.' The train is the only artificial interference, by Time.

Is this a book for now? Decidedly, yes. And for the 'now' not only of already avowed readers of Miss Compton-Burnett.

Parents and Children, coming at this juncture, is a book with which new readers might well begin. Miss Compton-Burnett, as ever, makes a few concessions; she has not, like some of our writers, been scared or moralised into attempts to converge on the 'real' in life. But possibly, life has converged on her. Elizabethan implacability, tonic plainness of speaking, are not so strange to us as they were. This is a time for *hard* writers—and here is one.

New Statesman and Nation, 1941

Elizabeth Bowen

ELDERS AND BETTERS

THE GREAT VICTORIAN novelists did not complete their task, their survey of the English psychological scene. One by one they died; their century ended, a decade or two before its nominal close. Then—as after one of those pauses in conversation when either exhaustion or danger is felt to be in the air—the subject was changed.

There came, with the early 1900's, a perceptible lightening, if a decrease in innocence: the Edwardian novelists were more frivolous, more pathetic. Their dread of dowdiness and longwindedness was marked; content to pursue nothing to its logical finish, they reassured their readers while amusing them, and restored at least the fiction of a *beau monde*. They were on the side of fashion: to shine, for their characters, was the thing. Competent, nervous, and in their time daring, they redecorated the English literary haunted house. Their art was an effort to hush things up. Curiously enough, in view of that, almost all the novels I was forbidden to read as a child were contemporary, which was to say, Edwardian. They were said to be 'too grown up'. (To the infinitely more frightening Victorians, no ban attached whatsoever: a possible exception was *Jane Eyre*.) When, therefore, I did, as I could hardly fail to, read those Edwardian novels, I chiefly got the impression of being left out of something enjoyable. Here was life no longer in terms of power, as I as a child had seen it, but in terms of illusion for its own sake, of successful performance, of display. Yes, and here the illusion bent on the grown-up state, on its stylishness, its esoteric quality. The fashions of the day, that I saw round me—artful silhouettes, intricate mounted hair-dressing, the roses, violets or cherries heaped high on hats—the constant laughter I heard in other rooms and the quick recourses, in my presence, to French, all contributed something to this. The Edwardians, perhaps to mark the belated accession of their King, did, however speciously, build up the grown-up idea. The distant existence of that *élite*, that group of performers that I approached so slowly and who might be no longer there by the time I reached them (a premonition which was to be justified) tormented me, in common with other children. I should like to know how the Edwardian novel affected its grown-up readers. In them too, I suppose, it played on the social nerve, the sensation of missing something.

That the Edwardians were, in fact, on the retreat, that they were fugitives from the preposterous English truths of Victorianism, putting up the best show they could, probably did not appear in their own day. Their shallowness was a policy, however unconscious. We owe it to them to see not only the speciousness but the ingeniousness of their contrived illusion. This was only not stronger because they were poor in artists: it reaches a worthy level in the best of the novels of E. F. Benson; it attains to a sublimation, nothing to do with fear, in the later novels of Henry James.

What, then, was this task the Victorians failed to finish, and that the Edwardians declined to regard as theirs? A survey of emotion as an aggressive force, an account of the battle for power that goes on in every unit of English middle-class life. The Victorians' realism and thoroughness, with regard to what interested them, has perhaps been underrated: where these do not operate, where they are superseded by jocose patter or apparent prudery, I think we may assume the Victorians' interest flagged—for instance, I think it arguable that they were not, imaginatively, interested in sex, and that they were hardly aware of society. Their blind spots matter less than their concentration, from which some few blind spots could not fail to result: they concentrated on power and its symbols—property, God, the family. Of these, their analysis was unconscious: the order was one to which they fully subscribed; they had no idea that they were analysing it, or that, carried far enough, this must be destructive. In that sense their innocence was complete.

For what they required to work on, for what magnetised them, the Victorians had no need to look far beyond the family. The family was the circuit: the compulsory closeness of its members to one another, like the voluntary closeness of people making a ring of contact to turn a table, generated something. Society was, for the Victorian novelists' purpose, comparatively negligible: as a concept they could and did ignore it; it might just exist as a looser outside ring, a supplementary system of awards and penalties, or an enlarged vague reproduction of the family pattern. Love was recognized as either promising an addition to the family structure by a right marriage, or threatening damage to it by a wrong one; apart from this, desire was sheer expense, and the lover from the outside, as a late-comer, must be either a nincompoop or a pirate. . . . This would seem to hold good of Dickens and Trollope (whose personal sociability committed them to nothing stronger in writing than a good word for a good time had with good fellows, and left them derisive about any *beau monde*) and of the Brontë sisters, for all their stress on the isolated passion of individuals. As to George Eliot it seems doubtful: her analysis was more conscious, which makes her less Victorian. The most obvious instance is Charlotte M. Yonge, and the major exception Thackeray, whose sense of society was acute, and whose families are in a felt relation to it.

Thackeray was in another sense an exception: in his novels there do exist grown-up people. For elsewhere, with the Victorians, we are in a world of dreadful empowered children. The rule of the seniors only is not questioned because, so visibly, they can enforce it; meanwhile, their juniors queue up, more or less impatiently awaiting their turn for power. The family gradations, though iron, are artificial: inwardly, everyone is the same age. The Victorians could not depict maturity because they did not believe in it. The father of the family was the extension of his youngest son's impotent buried wish, the mother, with her mysterious productivity, that of her daughter's daydream. How far the Victorian family was falsified by the mirror of Victorian art, or how far its characteristics were merely exaggerated, cannot be settled here: it is the art not the family that we study. For that matter, were the Victorian artists influenced by the passionate conjugality, and later equally passionate widowed seclusion, of their Queen? In its subjectivity, in its obsession with emotional power, the age was feminine: the assertions by the male of his masculinity, the propaganda for 'manliness' go to show it. The apronstring, so loudly denounced, was sought, and family life, through being ostensibly patriarchal, was able to cover much. Trollope, in whose own youthful experience family life had stood for debts and deathbeds, and Dickens, in whose it had stood for debts and disgrace, were active in forwarding the ideal.

Or, so it seemed to their readers and to themselves. It can be seen now that Victorian novel-writing, had it continued upon its course, would have endangered, not by frankness but by its innocent observations, the proprieties by which we must hope to live. It can be seen why the Edwardians took fright, and sought refuge in the society fairy-tale. It was certainly not the Edwardians who were the *enfants terribles*. As it happened, the Victorians were interrupted; death hustled them, one by one, from the room. We may only now realize that these exits, and, still more, the nervous change of subject that followed them, were a set-back for the genuine English novel. Its continuity seems to be broken up. Since then, we have a few brilliant phenomena, but, on the whole, a succession of false starts.

Have we, today, any serious novelist who has taken up, or even attempted to take up, at the point where the Victorians left off?

A possible answer might be, Miss Compton-Burnett, whose latest novel, *Elders and Betters*, calls for some fresh discussion of her position. She, like the Victorians, deals with English middle-class family life—her concentration on it is even more frankly narrow. In form, it is true, her novels are ultra-Edwardian; their pages present an attractive lightness, through all the weight being thrown on elliptical dialogue; but, beyond that, their unlikeness to the Edwardian is infinite—to begin and end with, they allow no place for illusion. They are, at the first glance, unlike the Victorian in being static (time is never a factor in them), in being unsensuous and unvisual, in refusing to differentiate between comedy and tragedy, in being without remorse. They resemble the Victorian in their sedateness, and in their atmosphere of physical and social security. Her avoidance of faked, or outward, Victorianism, however, is marked: we find ourselves with this, and more, guarantees that Miss Compton-Burnett is not merely copying but actually continuing the Victorian novel.

She continues it, that is to say, from the inside. Her being in the succession shows in her approach to her subject, rather than in her choice of it—for the family as a subject has never been out of fashion; there is no question of its being reinstated. What Miss Compton-Burnett revives is a way of seeing; she sees, with hyper-acute vision, what the Victorians saw, and what they had still to see. She has been too clever, or too instinctively wise, to set her novels inside any stated time: the idiom of talk is modern, the way of living dates from thirty to forty years back. Costume and accessories play so little part that her characters sometimes give the effect of being physically, as well as psychologically, in the nude, and of not only standing and moving about in but actually sitting on thin air. For some reason, this heightens their reality. In space, they move about very little: they go for short walks, which generally have an object, or advance on each other's houses in groups, like bomber formations. They speak of what they will do, and what they have done, but are seldom to be watched actually doing it—in *Elders and Betters*, we do see Anna burning the will: on examination, we find this to be necessary, for this act she will not admit, and so can never describe. . . . This bareness, which starves the reader's imagination and puts the whole test of the plot to his intellect is, surely, un-Victorian? Miss Compton-Burnett has stripped the Victorian novel of everything but its essentials—which must have been fewer than we thought. Her interest is in its logic, which she applies anew.

As a title, *Elders and Betters* is ironical: everyone in this novel is the same age, and nobody is admirable. In a Victorian novel, the characters fail to impose upon the reader; here, they fail to impose upon each other. The revolution, foreseeable, long overdue, has arrived—without disturbing a single impalpable cup on the impalpable drawing-room mantelpiece. It has been succeeded by this timeless anarchy, in which meals are served and eaten, visits paid, engagements to marry contracted and broken off. Everything that was due to happen in the world the Victorians posited, and condoned, has happened—but, apparently, there is still more to come: such worlds are not easily finished with, and Miss Compton-Burnett may not see the finish herself. For one thing, that disrespect for all other people underlying Victorian manners (as Victorians showed them) has not yet come to the end of its free say, and fear has not yet revenged itself to the full. The passive characters, almost all young men, marvel at the others, but not much or for long; they return to marvelling at themselves. Only the callous or those who recuperate quickly can survive, but in *Elders and Betters* everyone does survive—except Aunt Jessica, who commits suicide after the scene with Anna. In this we are true to the masters; in the Victorian novel people successfully die of their own death-wishes (as Aunt Sukey dies in *Elders and Betters*), but nobody ever dies of an indignity.

Miss Compton-Burnett shows, in *Elders and Betters*, that she can carry weight without losing height. She has been becoming, with each novel, less abstract, more nearly possible to enclose in the human fold. *Elders and Betters* is, compared, for instance, with *Brothers and Sisters, terre à terre*; but with that I greet a solid gain in effect. The more she masters what I have called her logic, the more material she can use. Her technique for melodrama has been by degrees perfected, and is now quite superb: I know nothing to equal Chapter X of this book—the duel in Aunt Sukey's death-chamber, after Aunt Sukey's death. Only second to this is the lunch-party, at which two families voice their disgust at old Mr Calderon's engagement to Florence, the governess's young niece. There is an advance, too (again, a logical one), in the articulateness of employed persons: nothing protects the Donnes against Cook and Ethel, with whom even Anna is placatory. The importance of money has not budged, but dependence is now felt by the monied side—also, there is, with regard to employed persons, either a weakening or a belated dawn of grace. In one of the earlier novels, it seemed consistent that a child of the house should laugh every time the governess eats; in *Elders and Betters*, a child suffers because he has left a governess out in the dusk and rain. And religion, the worship in the rock garden, for the first time enters the scene.

The post-Victorian novel, in Miss Compton-Burnett's hands, keeps its course parallel with our modern experience, on which it offers from time to time, a not irrelevant comment in its own language. To the authority of the old, relentless tradition, it has added an authority of its own.

Cornhill Magazine, 1944

John Betjeman

A FATHER AND HIS FATE

To REVIEW NOVELS of Miss Ivy Compton-Burnett among other fiction, English or American, is rather like having to describe an etching in an exhibition of oil paintings. It is analogous, but not the same.

A Father and His Fate is like the other fourteen novels Miss Compton-Burnett has published. It is written about people who live in fairly affluent circumstances in the country, probably the West Country, and the time when the events occur is somewhere about 1894 or 1895, judging from internal evidence.

Description of scenery, of rooms and houses, and even of the many characters themselves, is almost wholly lacking. The characters describe themselves by what they say. Indeed, when Miss Compton-Burnett stoops to describe the looks of one of them, one feels she regards these as unimportant, and that they might as well have been left out.

All the characters speak in the same language. For instance, a daughter of the house says to the manservant:

'So you were prepared to leave us, Everard?'
'Well, Miss, I did not instigate it. It was the idea that my office was a sinecure.'
'I should have thought that might be a pleasant one.'
'I have feelings, Miss. And self-respect is not absent.'

The only colour Miss Compton-Burnett allows her novels is in their plots, and these are usually melodramatic. *A Father and His Fate* is no exception, and concerns two related families, one with three unmarried daughters and appendages, and the other with three unmarried sons.

You might think that a novel consisting almost entirely of conversation—and conversation on the same note—would be unreadable. And many people find Miss Compton-Burnett's work not to their taste. But her steadily growing band of admirers read her because she is the essence of wit.

There may be funnier writers, but I doubt if there is a wittier writer living than she. Moreover, the plots by their very sensationalism serve to show up the wit of the calm conversation that discusses the dramatic events:

> 'I wonder if there is anyone in the world who cares for me,' said Miles, leaning back in his chair. 'I often ask myself that question.'
> 'Then you should answer it,' said Ursula. 'It is less safe to put it to other people.'

Whether you care for Miss Compton-Burnett is something you can only find out for yourself.

Daily Telegraph, August 16, 1957

R. Glynn Grylls

A FATHER AND HIS FATE

ADMIRERS OF Miss Compton-Burnett's books who have listened
to the latest one broadcast on the Third Programme (three times
before publication—surely a thing to stand by itself?) cannot but
have felt that some nuances were lost, some subtleties blunted,
admirably as it was done. To read after hearing has had its own
keener edge of enjoyment.

What is *A Father and His Fate* about? It is about the struggle for
existence, the threat of the jungle, the lust for power to which love
and death come poor seconds: that is, like any other novel by
Miss Compton-Burnett, it is about a family whose address is
'Huis Clos'. In this instance the story has to do with a father who
thinks he is widowed and wants to marry again but whose wife
reappears before he can do so.

From this, themes enough arise: a mother's jealousy of her
daughter-in-law, children's jealousy of an interloper, everyone's
unworthy reaction to bereavement. The eternal conflict of wills
within a family group comes to a climax in the manoeuvring for
the seat of power at the tea-table: a brilliant scene. And with it
goes the convention of that talk where every sentence is sifted and
the setting in which the same characters are shown in their infinite
variety.

The father here is a bullying head of family like Horace Lamb
in *Manservant and Maidservant* and Cassius Clare in *The Present and
the Past*, and his wife disappears and returns like Harriet Haslam
in *Men and Wives*, but they are completely different. The support-
ing characters are less fully developed than in other books (for this
one is very short) so that the butler, Everard, for instance, is only
a shadow of Buttermere and Bullivant. But a new type of personality is presented in Verena, a young woman of open ruthlessness: 'she knows how to serve herself'.

I must admit that the clue to this on her entry escapes me, as
does the significance of her name, given in full as Verena Eliza

Gray. And names are at the heart of the Compton-Burnett mystery. From the girls called Dolores and Felicity in her very first novel (*Dolores*, published 1911; the vintage years began in 1929) she arrived at the two cats of *Mother and Son*, 1955, whose names, Plautus and Tabbikin, reveal the families which own them.

Miss Compton-Burnett on cats marked a superb year: not that felinity lacks here. The authentic note is struck and sustained throughout and there is a fitting, final irony when the sister-in-law who always knows everything is left not knowing the most important fact of all.

Sunday Times, August 11, 1957

John Preston

A HERITAGE AND ITS HISTORY

MUCH OF THE criticism of Ivy Compton-Burnett's novels sounds as if it is intended for club members. Indeed, it often seems to arise from the assumption that the novels are specifically written for a select minority audience, that they are 'altered' versions of the standard product for those 'in the know'. So, for instance, character and the action that reveals character will be dominant in these as in other novels. The difference is that you have to deduce characteristics that are hidden behind the witty and un-modulated dialogue. This is a game one soon tires of, especially as the range of character-invention is very circumscribed. There are understandably many readers who think it not worth the candle.

Yet it should be obvious that Ivy Compton-Burnett has very little use for people. She can of course be acute about them; but the important thing is that she will not allow a novel to grow out of the experience of her characters. She breaks the connec-tion between character and action, forcing us to see both as arbitrary and motiveless. An example of this is at the end of *Elders and Betters*, where the men and women of two families find themselves scrambling for partners in marriage. The manoeuvres are, it is true, prompted by personal feelings, but they cannot be said to express or enrich personality. On the con-trary, the scene reads like a calculated insult to human feeling. One of the characters involved says:

> Oh, all of them seem to be tumbling helter-skelter along the road of the life-force. It seems odd to make an open parade of it. You would think it would be a matter for the individual soul. Or the individual something; I don't know that the soul has much to do with it. It all seems rather unreticent and primitive somehow. I suppose I am over-civilised or something (Ch. 13, p. 210).

The words 'unreticent', 'primitive', 'over-civilised' are impor-tant. They take us directly to a central theme of all the novels:

people evolve social forms in order to insulate themselves against primitive forces, the unknown or, worse, the 'unmentionable'. For, of course, language is one, perhaps the most effective, of these social forms. We can persuade ourselves that what is not said does not exist; alternatively, that the proper function of words is to express social sanctions and relationships, not to speak truth. This should suggest a readjustment of our view of the novels. They offer a linguistic rather than a psychological scrutiny of human experience. 'I thought it put the matter in a word', says a character in her most recent novel, *A Heritage and Its History*.

> 'Yes, that is what it did. But is a word the right vehicle for any-thing with such a range, nothing less than the whole of human destiny?'
> 'Words are all we have. It is no good to find fault with them' (Ch. 2, p. 38).

It is no good to find fault with words, but it is essential to find what fault there is in them. It may amount to little more than the jargon of the school notice-board: 'Observe silence in passages and on stairs.' The boys are told that 'observe' means 'keep'; they read the other notices:

> '. . . 'Observe punctuality at meals' . . . '*Keep* punctuality at meals?' said Holland, as if to himself.
> (*Two Worlds and Their Ways*, Ch. 4, p. 144)

But a passage in *Manservant and Maidservant* lays more stress on the social pressures behind such linguistic devaluation. The illiterate Miss Buchanan, whose shop serves as a *poste restante*, is asked about her 'clientèle'. The word has to be explained to her:

> 'the people who avail themselves of your services' . . .
> 'those who resort to your facilities' . . .
> 'or who receive any kind of attention from you.'
> 'Oh, those who want to hide their letters,' said Miss Buchanan, as though a more pedestrian term would have been in place (Ch. 8, p. 154).

It would not, of course, have been 'in place'. But Miss Buchanan's illiteracy is proof against these 'accommodations' in language. Like the schoolboys, she has a kind of linguistic innocence.

Other characters have only too great a facility with words. Emotional dishonesty, emotional tyranny, an oppressive egocentricity: these are characteristics that Ivy Compton-Burnett examines again and again. They are the attributes particularly associated with this manipulation of language. We hear from these characters the voice of power. Its accents are derived from the whole social tone, and this is its strength: there can be no appeal against it without weakening the insulating layer of speech.

Miles, in *A Father and His Fate*, speaks with this voice: his emotional self-indulgence imposes obligations:

> 'My dear ones, my own even dearer ones,' said Miles, as he embraced his daughters, 'my poor, motherless girls! . . . Your father returns to you alone. But remember what you will do for him, what you have already done. . . . We shall tread the empty road together . . .'
>
> (Ch. 6, p. 86).

It is later made quite clear that we are to see this as primarily a linguistic matter. Miles, on the point of marrying for a second time, is told that his first wife is still alive; in his reply 'his voice came low and even, almost as if he were quoting what he said' (Ch. 8, p. 142). The reunion with his wife and her restoration to the family he makes into a linguistic victory:

> 'Yes,' said Miles, 'it is a full and fit reward. Sorrow, mistakes and mistaken effort are all wiped away.'
>
> 'So uncle accepts his deserts,' said Malcolm to Ursula. 'But I wish he would not talk about them.'
>
> 'It is the best thing he could do. I was afraid of silence . . .'
>
> . . . 'You are silent, my wife,' said Miles. 'But your silence speaks. We do not need your words. We know what is in your heart, as we feel the echo in our own.'
>
> 'With uncle something else speaks,' said Malcolm. 'Not silence.'
>
> (Ch. 11, p. 145)

Rhetoric makes the man impregnable. A glib tongue is the mark of social solidity. At this point the linguistic evaluation (which is a moral one) works through hilarious and ruthless mimicry.

To counterbalance those characters who use language for

camouflage there are those who speak out. Sabine does so, in *Daughters and Sons*: 'I do not care to have a member of my house with a dull complexion and a dull manner and a dull face' (Ch. 1, p. 7). Hers is an unguarded, a more vulnerable tone. It is not far from impotent rage: her voice becomes 'shrill and strained' (Ch. 7, p. 195). And in general the tyrant's insults do no damage to the crust of social form. They are outspoken but not true.

There is a more disquieting form of plain speaking in the novels. It undermines the language that solidifies the conventions and evasions and prejudices of a social group. Things no longer 'go without saying'; what is generally held or asserted is now to be re-examined. 'But people are ashamed of the oddest things . . . though they are supposed only to be proud of them.' 'It is so untrue that to the pure all things are pure. They are particularly impure, of course' (*Two Worlds and Their Ways*, Ch. 5, pp. 125–6). People who do not need the support of social forms, the weak, the bitter, the self-defeated, are best placed to threaten the entrenched positions of language. They speak with a caustic honesty as damaging to pretentiousness as it is mortifying to their self-respect. In *Manservant and Maidservant* Horace, the head of a household, domineering and ruthless, is exposed in this way by his cousin and dependent, Mortimer. Horace learns that his wife and Mortimer are in love. The scene in which he tells Mortimer to leave the house produces a naked opposition between the two kinds of speech:

> 'You have been a good friend to me, Mortimer, or rather you have been a dear one. But you have cut the ground from under our feet. Now that we both begin again, in remorse for the past, in amended lives, we cannot do it together. In future we go forward apart.'
> 'Just as our mutual influence would be so good. We seem only to have had the worst of each other. And how am I to go forward?'
> 'You can help yourself, and there are others who will help you. I will do my best for you, though you have not done yours for me.'
> 'Well, I must leave it to you and the others. You are in a beautiful place. I do not wonder you talk about it. It must be wonderful to have power, and use it with moderation and cruelty. We can so seldom be admired and self-indulgent at the same time.' (Ch. 6, p. 120.)

This offers the confrontation of two modes of being, rather than the collision between two personalities. At least we do not care much about either speaker as a person, though it is fascinating to note how the very natural, rancorous tones emerge from the impassive sentences. Our attention is caught by the abstract words, 'remorse', 'influence', 'power', 'moderation', 'cruelty'. The opposition seems to belong to the words rather than to the persons; the modes of being are rendered as modes of speech.

Mortimer rebels against Horace, but he needs him also. '"It is a humbling thought," said Mortimer, "We are Horace's slaves in soul. We belong to him and not to ourselves"' (Ch. 13, p. 228). Mortimer's honesty is relatively ineffectual. He forces language to recognise the unpleasant, but still excludes 'the unmentionable'. Language is an instrument of social cohesion and of social rebellion; it is also the only way of facing the unknown. It is necessary 'to say it once. Then it is faced and said' (*A Father and His Fate*, Ch. 11, p. 150). When Miles's daughters have to tell him of their mother's return, they find that it almost goes beyond what can be 'faced and said'. 'It is the worst thing to have to embarrass him. And this is embarrassment on such a scale. We seem to want a stronger word' (*Ibid.*, Ch. 10, p. 139). 'Embarrassment on such a scale': some experience tears a gaping hole in the social fabric. Language is mostly used as Miles himself uses it, to deflect the experience. But sometimes language is an instrument of truth and forces us to engage with the experience.

It is not only language that must bear the strain of such experience. Language, we have seen, is only one part of social behaviour. Ivy Compton-Burnett writes of a world in which social forms are rigid and important, almost a ritual. Her characters care deeply about the proper conduct of the tea-table, about precedence, about the domestic hierarchy. This elaborate and systematised social demeanour clearly serves, like the language that goes with it, to shield the civilised life against unmanageable or 'embarrassing' experiences.

In *Elders and Betters* there is an extended and richly comic scene (Ch. 6) in which high civilisation is brought face to face with superstitious fear: '"Thirteen at the table!" said Tullia, checking herself as she was about to sit down.' This releases a flood of talk as the standing people try to hide their fear from themselves and from each other. The situation is wonderfully exploited as they discover that, successively, 'it is the *last* person who sits down, who takes the risk', they are fourteen at table, it is perhaps 'the person who *gets up* last who dies in a short time', they really are fourteen. The scene is masterly, one of the finest in all Ivy Compton-Burnett's novels. And it is centrally important. The dinner-table is one of the most obvious and telling ways in which society refines a simple biological need into a ceremony. Yet here, at the very point where the ceremony seems most secure, a sort of primitive terror breaks through. Far from assimilating this terror, the civilised life seems, by repressing it, to have made it more damaging. The social rituals are a sort of propitiation, like the children's worship, in the same novel, of their personal god, Chung. When their cousin is allowed to participate in this, he feels as he does 'after stirring a wish into the Christmas pudding, that if there were anything in these problematic forces, they could now only operate in his favour' (Ch. 6, p. 98).

In *A Heritage and Its History*, all these preoccupations are presented more completely and explicitly than ever before. The book would suggest, if such a thing could seem possible, a final statement. The 'heritage' gives a hold on the 'civilised' world; its 'history', its continuity is a way of defying death. 'And life and death may be called primitive,' as the butler, Deakin, observes (Ch. 3, p. 51). Yet the heritage is itself deathly; it is presented in a symbol:

> 'The creeper on the house, Mater,' said Simon. 'I said it should be cut down.' . . .
> 'But what is wrong with the creeper? It adds so much to the house.'
> 'Too much,' said Simon. 'It throws its shadow all over it. This room is like a dungeon. I should be thankful to see it gone.'
> 'I should be most distressed. It is part of my home to me, of the background of my married life. It will not go with my consent.'
> (Ch. 1, p. 12)

The ageing Sir Edwin's tenacious hold on the heritage, on life itself, is indirectly the means of exposing his nephew, Simon, to an ungovernable instinctive force. Edwin's young wife, Rhoda, bears Simon's child; they both regard themselves as victims of an uncontrollable force ('It was fate, impulse, force') which has emerged as this because it was thwarted and repressed by Edwin's code: Simon pleads with Edwin:

> 'I can only say that youth and instinct did their work.'
> 'Our instincts are subject to us. That is saying nothing.'
>
> (Ch. 6, p. 101)

This divorce between instinctive and social behaviour is what sustains the social structure; and it is assisted by the power of the word, a power greater than truth. Edwin declares that he himself will be known as the father of Simon's child:

> 'But—the boy is mine, Uncle. You and I know it, though others do not. We can only abide by our knowledge.'
> 'What you and I know is forgotten. The real truth is not the truth to us. We abide by the accepted word.'
>
> (Ch. 6, p. 139)

'We have to veil the truth,' Edwin maintains; and Simon acquiesces. His allegiance is to the heritage. He becomes himself an instrument of domestic tyranny.

There comes a time when Edwin's supposed son and Simon's daughter wish to marry. Simon is confronted with an even more threatening situation: 'You have been so much the master of them all, the mentor, the absolute head. It would all (i.e. if he were to reveal that the two were brother and sister) be seen as empty pose. Can you face it, and go on after it?' (Ch. 9, p. 157). But it is not only that the family tyrant faces exposure: the whole idea of the 'civilised life' is called in question. Edwin opposes the idea of revealing the truth about Simon's child:

> 'Civilised life exacts its toll. We live among the civilised.'
> 'The conventions are on the surface,' said his wife (Rhoda). 'We know the natural life is underneath.'
> 'We do, we have our reason. But we cannot live it. We know the consequence of doing so. If not, we learn.'
>
> (Ch. 9, p. 160)

In some days, Simon claims, the incestuous marriage they are trying to avert 'would have been lawful and right.'

'We live in our own,' said Sir Edwin.
'What Simon and I did, is done in all days,' said Rhoda.

(Ch. 9, p. 161)

This is the point to which the whole novel, indeed all the novels, have been driving. There is one character, a poet, who offers to do the difficult thing: '"Would you like me to say the word?" said Walter.' But it is Simon who says the word and who, in the process, seals the crack in the civilised life and finally secures the heritage for himself. 'Is the creeper on the house to be cut back?' said Deakin, the butler. 'Sir Simon dislikes it to encroach.'

'We will give it a respite, Deakin,' said Simon.
'Encroachment seems to be its work. And we are so inured to the shadow, that we might be startled by the light.'

(Ch. 13, p. 237)

The word may startle us by its light; it may also inure us to the shadow. Ivy Compton-Burnett makes the word the subject as it is the medium of her work. She puts 'the matter in a word' and we find that it is 'nothing less than the whole of human destiny'.

Essays in Criticism, July, 1960

Hilary Spurling

THE LAST AND THE FIRST

DAME IVY COMPTON-BURNETT's complete works—completed yesterday, on publication of her twentieth novel (*The Last and the First*)—will no doubt produce fresh entries in a reckoning by no means settled yet. On the one hand there are those who, like Nathalie Sarraute, hold Dame Ivy 'one of the greatest novelists England has ever had', and one of the very few in any language who have this century changed the novel, as the post-impressionists changed painting. On the other hand, there are those who find that—as Dame Ivy nicely said—'If you once pick up a Compton-Burnett, it is difficult not to put it down again.'

Admittedly, given the long and strong conservatism of the literary establishment, the two views are complementary. One may trace their fluctuations over fifty years or so of reviews in the *New Statesman*, always an expert guide to current fashion. An unknown author in 1925, she starts at the foot of a new novels column devoted largely to deflating Lawrence's *St Mawr*; indeed, a dim view of D. H. Lawrence takes up so much space that there is barely room to acknowledge the arrival of I. Compton-Burnett: 'As for *Pastors and Masters*, it is astonishing, alarming. It is like nothing else in the world. It is a work of genius.' Her next two books are dismissed with patronising terseness; David Garnett in 1933 is pleased but puzzled by 'this queer writer', and Raymond Mortimer in 1935 notes that the future of the English novel lies with Miss Compton-Burnett.

By the end of the Thirties—five books and twelve years later—she has reversed her position in the new novels column, and remains firmly at the top for the next quarter of a century. Other novelists (Elizabeth Bowen, P. H. Newby, V. S. Pritchett and V. S. Naipaul) contribute the shrewdest as well as the most appreciative reviews. Philip Toynbee in 1944 is the first to mention 'a sect of devotees' and 'a mystery cult' with which—having himself introduced the notion, and built it up on somewhat dubious grounds—he is the first to taunt her a few years later. *A God and His Gifts* (1963) was the last novel published in Dame Ivy's lifetime; and, given the admiration which had gone before, it was perhaps inevitably demolished by Brigid Brophy.

What is curious is not so much the fact of these assaults—a good many novelists, I daresay, would show over the same period the same pattern of slow rise and sudden fall—as their mood and content. Miss Brophy (whose tone is by no means untypical) writes with a vehemence which recalls Dame Ivy's Dr Cassell— 'He had so long interpreted a conversation as a didactic utterance by himself, that argument on equal terms struck him as deliberate baiting'—and it is not hard to see why. For Dame Ivy's detractors are well aware of revolutionary tendencies: their charge, which seldom varies, is in essence that she flouts strict nineteenth-century convention. Mr Toynbee's complaint is that she does not arouse in him the same emotion as Dostoevsky; Miss Brophy's that her technique is different from Jane Austen's. Their regular grievances—that she is unfeeling, inartistic and flagrantly unreal; that she can't draw character, or can't develop it; that she eschews narrative composition in favour of highly stylised designs—are, as Mr Mortimer pointed out in 1935, precisely those once laid against Cézanne.

So it is no wonder if a taste nurtured on the opulence of the nineteenth century—or, for that matter, on more recent English fiction, which might well lead one to suppose that development in the novel had stopped a very long time ago—finds Dame Ivy something of a shock. Her austerity, the abruptness of her plots, the formality of her dialogue, the fact that both are deployed with such conscious artifice, provoke a sense of outrage which distracts attention from what, in these books, is genuinely outrageous. This is, after all, not so much the unnatural polish of Dame Ivy's family conversation, rather the ruthlessness with which she probes its jagged underside. For the wit that decorates her pages in such gaiety and profusion is also strictly functional: a smooth veneer which splits and bulges under pressure from beneath, and which yet maintains a precarious surface tension. 'My rests,' said Mozart according to Busoni, 'are more important than my notes'; and 'There can be great silences', says a character in *The Last and the*

First, a saying which one may perhaps take as a sombre comment on her author. For, if the frivolity of the voices on the surface is constantly diverting, it is matched by a fearful sense of pain and perturbation, furtive thrust and shrinking impact which take place in silence far below.

Covert brutality, private hurt, the dangerously thin coating of civility over both, seem always to have preoccupied Dame Ivy; and anyone still puzzled as to why a twentieth-century novelist should need to jettison the stylistic trappings of an earlier school will find the answer strikingly laid out in Dame Ivy's very first novel, *Dolores.* Published in 1911, when she was twenty-seven, virtually suppressed thereafter and published once again this week, it could scarcely be more different from the nineteen novels which, after a gap of fourteen years, followed it in punctual succession. It is not simply that *Dolores* is a startlingly bad book; it is bad in ways that a weaker, more accommodating and potentially less original imagination might readily have avoided.

Dolores starts at a funeral, and it has been remarked that the tolling repetitions of this opening passage are modelled (like much else in this book) on George Eliot. What has not as yet been noticed is the strange fact that this first chapter—the open grave, the dreary day, the parsonage bordering the churchyard, the widower attended by his mourning parishioners, his sorrow and remorse—duplicates another funeral, identical in setting as in personnel. This is the final scene in 'The Sad Fortunes of the Reverend Amos Barton' from George Eliot's *Scenes of Clerical Life.* Indeed, George Eliot's Mr Barton might almost be said to walk again as Dame Ivy's Reverend Cleveland Hutton, just as his nineteen-year-old daughter Patty resembles, in all but name, 'the nine-year-old Dolores, with her mother's voice and her mother's form, and her fitting part in her mother's name of sorrows!'.

It can scarcely be coincidence that the end of George Eliot's first story should furnish forth the beginning of Dame Ivy's first novel; and considering what came later (for no two novelists are more dissimilar in mature achievement), it is illuminating to see why, in taking up the story where George Eliot stopped, Dame Ivy came signally to grief. In minor matters, *Dolores* faithfully follows 'Amos Barton': both are set back from the time of writing a quarter of a century or so (the only borrowing which Dame Ivy later kept); both assume the same uneasy intimacy with the reader, and both alternate between extreme solemnity and passages of vivid, mocking, comic observation. Dame Ivy's Millfield, with its teeming clerical life, abundant clergy, rival evangelists (among them the egregious Dr Cassell) vying for attention from argumentative and sharply critical parishioners, might be George Eliot's Shepperton forty or fifty years on. More interesting, perhaps, is the relationship between the second Mrs Hutton and her sister, Mrs Blackwood, which recalls the spats between the sisters Glegg, Dodson and Tulliver in *The Mill on the Floss*. Here Dame Ivy describes in the omniscient third person ('. . . the sisters' dialogue was charged with hidden currents. It became a series of thrusts with verbal weapons seemingly innocent, but carrying each its poisoned point') what, in her later books, she catches in the act. And already, in the conversation bounced like a ball from hand to hand at the Blackwoods' evening party, one may trace the tentative beginnings of a technique she was later to perfect.

But the book centres on Dolores, a heroine endowed with a sense of duty sterner and more casuistical than even Dorothea Casaubon's; and if the treatment of this theme suggests an academic copy— grandiose, lifeless and painfully stilted in execution—of George Eliot, it also explains why, having carried the naturalistic method to an extreme at once logical and ludicrous, Dame Ivy abandoned it forthwith. For Dolores' grotesque and secret torments ('Unfaceable pain', 'a surging of passion that paled her lips', 'she was saved from darkness only by the suffering need of living the surface life'), which cause abject misery to herself and in time to other people—so much so that her self-immolation comes unintentionally to look like cruelty—already suggest her author's preoccupation with subterranean areas of character not previously charted; together with the impossibility of exploring them by conventional means.

For the difference between this and the latter books is one of means, not ends. To turn from *Dolores* to *The Last and the First* is to turn from sham to real pain. It is also like moving from an overblown naturalistic painting to an abstract composition where the old descriptive formulae, grown flabby and effusive, are condensed into a matter of line, space and intersection. Conversation here presents the same bland surface: the tone is dry, the arrangement formal, the whole rinsed, as it were, in irony. The Heriot family, assembled at the breakfast-table, stab and parry one another with a graceful expertise born of lifelong practice. Hermia Heriot, proposing to leave home, confronts her family with an animosity no less virulent for being dispassionately expressed. From her composure, drawn taut over submerged hysteria, one may gauge the strength of the bonds she breaks: 'We saw them being assailed and wrenched apart,' says her younger brother Angus, and his language is absurd—but so, for that matter, is the enormity of what has just taken place. 'You might be a figure in history, corrupted by power. It is what you are, except that you are not in history,' says Angus later to his mother, and the high good humour with which both accept the saying is an acknowledgment also of its perfect truthfulness.

But the dynastic struggle in *The Last and the First* has entered a calm, even a comparatively genial phase. Selfishness is nonchalantly confounded when Hermia, worsted, routed and utterly done down, returns an act of self-denial whereby power is transferred smoothly to herself. This ending—accomplished by means of a conveniently large fortune—one may take perhaps as Dame Ivy's little joke prepared for the benefit of her readers who, having witnessed through her books so much desperate unhappiness, are left at last with one in which, as in a fairytale, they all lived happily ever after.

New Statesman, February 5, 1971

IV

THE ART OF ASSESSMENT

Robert Liddell

THE NOVELS OF I. COMPTON-BURNETT

THE INDEBTEDNESS OF Miss Compton-Burnett to Jane Austen is generously acknowledged. It is the mark of one of her insincere or self-complacent characters that he does not much care for Jane Austen's novels.

'What do you think of Miss Jane Austen's books, Jermyn,' said Dominic, 'if I may approach so great a man upon a comparatively flimsy subject?'
'Our row of green books with the pattern on the backs, Rachel?' said Sir Percy with a sense of adequacy in conversation. 'Very old-fashioned, aren't they?'
'What do the ladies think of the author, the authoress, for she is of their own sex?' said Dominic.
'I have a higher standard for greatness,' said Agatha, 'but I don't deny she has great qualities. I give her the word great in that sense.'
'You put that very well, Mrs Calkin,' said Dominic. 'I feel I must become acquainted with the fair writer.'

The world that the two novelists depict is normally a limited one, the families at the big house, the rectory, and one or two other houses in an English village. Their social world ranges from a baronet to a respectable upper servant. In *Pastors and Masters* Miss Compton-Burnett has drawn a very vivid picture of a preparatory-school, but in her women's college in *Dolores* or her girls' school in *More Women than Men* little more education is shown taking place than in Mrs Goddard's school in *Emma*; she has chosen the school simply as an example (like the family) of a group of people living too closely together. The men in her books are doctors or clergy, or are present for long week-ends—having work in London and outside the books—or else they have retired from their professions, or never had any. 'Their professions and occupations are indicated', she says in the *Conversation*, 'but I am concerned with their personal lives; and following them into their professional world would lead to the alternations between two spheres, that I think is a mistake in books. I always regret it in the great Victorian novelists, though it would be hard to avoid it in books on a large scale.'

Why has she chosen this world, and why has she dated the action of her books some time between 1888 and 1902?*

Not out of a desire to imitate—Jane Austen is inimitable, and Miss Compton-Burnett has a very original mind. Nor has she acted out of nostalgia for a quiet, old-fashioned world: there is nothing quaint about her work, any more than there is about Miss Austen's—no period properties and no local colour.

She herself claims that she is accepting her limitations: 'I do not feel that I have any real or organic knowledge of life later than about 1910. I should not write of later times with enough grasp or confidence. I think this is why many writers tend to write of the past. When an age is ended, you see it as it is. And I have a dislike, which I cannot explain, of dealing with modern machinery and inventions. When war casts its shadow, I find that I recoil.'

Such a recognition of her range is in itself admirable, but it is impossible not to see more than that in the limitations within which she works. She is writing the pure novel, as Jane Austen did, concentrating upon human beings and their mutual reactions. So rare is such concentration in the English novel that any writer who conscientiously practises it is almost sure to be accused of 'imitating Jane Austen' whether their minds are alike or not: and the minds of Miss Austen and Miss Compton-Burnett are in many ways alike.

The isolation of her characters (and in all her novels except *Dolores* and *More Women than Men* there is strict unity of place) brings them into clearer relief, and enables their creator to do her real business, the study and revelation of human nature, with greater freedom. This isolation of the characters, and their lack of interest in social conditions outside the family, or in economic problems apart from those of the family fortunes, is made more credible by isolating them in time as well as in place—situating them in a period when the impact of public events on private

* The events of *Pastors and Masters* take place after 1918: this is the one exception.

individuals was less immediate and crushing than at present. Therefore she has chosen the end of Queen Victoria's reign. A few years earlier, and she would have been obliged to weight down her books with the trappings of the historical novel: as it is, she has obtained a liberating absence of contemporaneity at the small cost of substituting carriages for cars.

As if to boast of her freedom, her references to Politics are deliberately and engagingly flat. 'So you see, Parliament thought that Bill a wrong one, and it was thrown out,' Mr Burgess observes to one of his pupils in *Pastors and Masters*; and Duncan Edgeworth in *A House and Its Head* asks: 'You don't think this election business will follow that course?'

Miss Compton-Burnett has freed herself from all irrelevances in order to write the pure novel. And like Miss Austen she has a dislike for merely descriptive writing, which she uses with even greater economy.* The village which is to be the scene of action is undescribed and, except for Moreton Edge in *Brothers and Sisters*, is not even named. Characters are often tersely but completely described, in terms which do not remain in the memory, and it is necessary to turn back if we wish to remind ourselves of their appearance.

'Duncan Edgeworth was a man of medium height and build, appearing both to others and himself to be tall. He had narrow, grey eyes, stiff, grey hair and beard, a solid, aquiline face, young for his sixty-six years, and a stiff, imperious bearing. His wife was a small, spare, sallow woman, a few years younger, with large, kind, prominent eyes, a long, thin, questioning nose, and a harried, innocent, somehow fulfilled expression.'

One is inclined to wonder if much would be lost by the suppression of such passages. The author herself observes in the *Conversation*: 'I am sure that everyone forms his own conceptions, that are different from everyone else's, including the author's.'

* She will introduce cushions, like an easily portable stage-property, as an emblem of prosperity. Peter (in *Brothers and Sisters*) spills his tea over Sophia's cushions. Sabine Ponsonby (in *Daughters and Sons*) puts out cushions only when visitors are expected. Hope Cranmer (in *Parents and Children*) has cushions, and the Marlowes haven't.

Dialogue, to which in *Emma* Jane Austen had begun to give a far more important place, is the staple of this writer's work. It is a dialogue of a power and brilliance unmatched in English prose fiction. In her early and immature book, *Dolores*, the machine creaked audibly at times, but already functioned with precision. The style of that book is crude, bare and rather alarming. It is not like real English: it is like the language of translation. It reminds one of English translations of Russian novels and of Greek tragedy, and one may conjecture that both of them had formed an important part of her reading. Such a style is uneuphonious and harsh, but conscientiously renders a meaning—and that is what, like a translator, Miss Compton-Burnett already did, with a remarkable exactitude.

This ungainly, but precise language was later evolved into a dialogue, more dramatic than narrative, which, whether in longer speeches, or in the nearest equivalent in English to Greek tragic stichomythia, is an unrealistic but extraordinarily intense vehicle for the characters' thoughts and emotions, and enables their creator to differentiate them sharply, and, whenever she wishes, to condemn them out of their own mouths. Its nearness to or remoteness from ordinary spoken language will vary from place to place. There is no single formula that will cover it, and the author has indicated that no kind of 'figure in the carpet' is to be sought: 'it is simply the result of an effort to give the impression I want to give.'

'The key', says one critic, 'is the realisation that her characters speak precisely as they are thinking.' This key will not unlock more than a part of her work: part of the utterances of her good characters, and the utterances of exceptionally simple or straightforward characters.

For she excels particularly at the revelation of insincerity on all its levels: from that of characters who tell flat lies, to that of characters who have deceived themselves into believing what they say. In between are characters such as Dominic Spong, who are more than half-aware and are wholly tolerant of their own smarminess and their own insincere ways of talking: 'if I may approach so great a man upon a comparatively flimsy subject.'

Her idiom sometimes approximates to what one might actually

say if one were in the character's skin and situation, but also to what one might think and conceal; to what one might think of saying and bite back; to what one might afterwards wish one had said; to what one would like other people to think; and to what one would like to think oneself. It is unlikely that these alternatives are exclusive. A full analysis, with the necessary illustrations, would require the full-length book that should be written on Miss Compton-Burnett's work.

A resemblance to Jane Austen may be noted in the use of stilted or unmeaning language to indicate a bad or insincere character. The pretentious vulgarity of Mrs Elton with her 'Caro Sposo' or 'Hymen's saffron robe', the frigid pomposity of Sir Edward Denham's thoughts on the Novel, or of General Tilney's compliments to Catherine Morland have frequent parallels—generally in the speech of characters who pride themselves on their superior sensitiveness, subtlety, public spirit, or culture.

A speech of Dulcia Bode in *A House and Its Head* contains many of the worst horrors pilloried by Fowler in *Modern English Usage*. Fowler shows that such faults are not merely faults of expression, but generally spring from real faults in feeling and character; they are not merely due to faulty taste, but to moral faults—insincerity, vanity, cowardice, and more.

'Now, Mother dear, lift up your head and your heart. Mr Edgeworth has not roused himself from his own shock and sorrow—yes, and shame; for it must be almost that—to point us in our direction, without looking for a touch of resilience and response. We can best repay him by throwing up our heads, facing the four winds squarely, and putting our best foot foremost out of the morass, and also out of his house.'

Here are BATTERED ORNAMENTS, HACKNEYED PHRASES, IRRELEVANT ALLUSION, MIXED METAPHOR and FACETIOUS ZEUGMA. Elsewhere in the utterances of this irrepressible character are POLYSYLLABIC HUMOUR ('I suspect I shall come by a good deal of refreshment in the course of my peregrinations'), SUPERIORITY ('if I may be Irish') and many other atrocities.

Dulcia, however, is not a mere Slipslop or Malaprop, but a very penetrating delineation of an unsubtle and insensitive nature given to uncontrolled self-dramatization, and to the dramatization of her environment. Many other characters betray themselves by their speech, and some in ways too subtle to be illustrated by a brief citation. This feature of her style, alone, would make Miss Compton-Burnett a most remarkable writer.

Besides the terse descriptions of characters there are a few short descriptions of action, or brief paragraphs of introduction or transition, such as the exquisitely phrased entrance of Miss Charity Marcon in *Daughters and Sons*.

> Miss Charity Marcon walked up her garden path, crossed her hall and entered her plain little drawing-room, her great height almost coinciding with the door, and her long neck bending, lest the experience of years should prove at fault and it should quite coincide with it.

Since the short study *Pastors and Masters*, published in 1925 after a fourteen years' silence, Miss Compton-Burnett has been completely mistress of her unique style, which she has used in increasing perfection in the novels that have followed. The texture is so close and dramatic that quotation of isolated passages is almost impossible without leaving a misleading impression. The detachment by reviewers of some of her comic passages, which are the most easily quotable, has perhaps tended to give the impression that she is only a humorous writer, and to obscure the fact, intensely humorous though she often is, that her ironic view of family life is also serious, and even tragic.

Miss Austen drew family tyranny in two characters: General Tilney in *Northanger Abbey* and Mrs Norris in *Mansfield Park*. After her time family life went into a darker period. Victorian parents (though there were charming people among them) sometimes identified themselves with God, and modelled their behaviour towards their children upon that of Jehovah towards the Children of Israel at their most recalcitrant—and they claimed divine authority for their worst excesses. Theobald and Christina in *The Way of All Flesh* are terrifying family tyrants: they are closely drawn from Samuel Butler's own parents. Novels of the period are full of fearful autocracy, approved by the Victorian authors. There are plenty of memoirs to substantiate the evidence with genuine atrocity stories. Even in our own century, when the bonds of family life have been greatly relaxed, the domestic dictator still horribly flourishes. You would not believe what goes on behind the façade of many a comfortable family residence. Those whose own lives have been happy in this respect, are shocked and incredulous when they obtain an insight into the terrors of family life as it can be lived. As one of Miss Compton-Burnett's characters observes: 'people do not know about families.'

The subject-matter of all her books—tyranny in family life—is therefore neither unreal nor unimportant. On the contrary, it is one of the most important that a novelist could choose. The desire for domination, which in a dictator can plunge the world into misery, can here be studied in a limited sphere. The courage of those who resist dictation, and the different motives which cause people to range themselves on the side of the dictator can be minutely studied. In avoiding contemporary chatter about public events, Miss Burnett has gone instead to the heart of the matter: her works provide one with more penetrating social criticism than all propagandist fiction put together. The moral is this—and it is both edifying and beautiful—if a novelist refuses to be seduced by the clamour of contemporary fashion into a dissertation upon economics, politics, the philosophy of history or the like, and if he is true to his calling, which is the study of human nature, then all these other things will be given to him. He will inevitably be a social critic, a philosopher of history.

In each of the novels there is a tyrant; family tyranny is always an important, usually the most important theme. In *Dolores* the selfish claims of Cleveland Hutton are always liable to break up the academic career which his daughter has made for herself—in this youthful book her self-sacrifice is regarded as noble: in the later books it would have been thought horrible. In *Pastors and Masters* Henry Bentley, another clergyman, makes his children the victims of his nervous depression. In *Brothers and Sisters* Sophia Stace, and in *Men and Wives* Harriet Haslam are tyrannical and devouring mothers, though they differ from each other in their aims and methods, and their mental make-up.

The following scene, between Sophia Stace, her children and
their former nurse, on the evening after her husband's funeral, is
one of the author's finest comic scenes, but it is merely comic only
to those who are too insensitive to see that the family tyrant is as
evil as the dictator, and ethically far less easily defensible.

'I don't know whether you like sitting there, having your dinner,
with your mother eating nothing? On this day of all days! I don't
know if you have thought of it.'
'Oh, I understood that you wouldn't have anything,' said Patty,
rising and hurrying to her side with food. 'I am sure I thought you
said that.'
'I may have said those words,' said Sophia. 'It is true that I do not
want anything. I hardly could, could I? But I may need it. It may be
all the more necessary for me, for that reason. I don't think I should
be left without a little pressing today, sitting here, as I am, with my
life emptied. I hardly feel you should let me depend quite on myself.'
Her children's power of rising to such demand was spent. Patty
pressed food with a simply remorseful face.
'No, I will not have anything,' said Sophia, with her eyes on the
things in a way that gave Dinah one of her glimpses of her mother as
pathetic. 'Nobody minds whether I do or not; and that would be the
only thing that would persuade me, somebody's caring. I can't make
the effort alone.'
'Here, come, try some of this,' said Dinah. 'It is so light you can
get it down without noticing.'
'And this, and this,' said Andrew, coming forward with a dish in
each hand, and an air of jest.
'Darlings!' said Sophia, taking something from Dinah. 'Dear
ones! Yes, I will try to eat a little to please you. Let me have something from you, my Andrew. I will do my best.'

Josephine Napier, in *More Women than Men*, is a more subtle
type of tyrant, who is able to lead as well as drive her family and
colleagues into obedience; she is the most attractive and the most
dangerous of the tyrants, and the only one who combines that role
with murder. Duncan Edgeworth, in *A House and Its Head*, has the
superior honesty and directness of the male oppressor, but his
oppression is the more open and ruthless. In *Daughters and Sons*,
the matriarch, Sabine Ponsonby, and her unbalanced daughter,

Hetta, both tyrannise over their household. In *A Family and a Fortune*, Matilda Seaton tries to tyrannise over her richer relations, and succeeds in making the life of her paid companion impossible. The tyranny of the grandfather, Sir Jesse Sullivan, in *Parents and Children*, and of the invalid aunt, Sukey Donne, in *Elders and Betters* come less in the middle of the picture of those two books, and yet are the cause of most of the happenings.

In most cases it is the economic dependence of other people upon them that enables the tyrants to exercise their shocking power—but this is not always the case. Some people who are not economically dependent submit to it, because they are bound in affection to others who are economically dependent, and therefore wish to live in the tyrant's house. And of course Miss Compton-Burnett is too subtle to accept the economic explanation as the only one. In some cases it has nothing to do with the question. Three of her tyrannical aunts hold no purse strings, and one of them is, on the contrary, a poor relation, a dependant—at any rate as far as extra comforts are concerned—on the family which she dominates by her will. Such was the position of Mrs Norris in *Mansfield Park*.

Tyranny in the family generates a tense electric atmosphere in which anything might happen. Every thought, however outrageous, is given full and clear expression—for not only do the tyrants say exactly what they think, so, oddly, do their victims as well. The equivalent of the play-scenes in *Mansfield Park* are invested with the grimness of the play-scenes in *Hamlet*. A family conversation at the breakfast-table is so pregnant with horror, that one feels things cannot go on like this for long; the storm must break some time. One is quite right, it does break. This may happen in one of two ways, but there will probably be violent happenings. It is the great distinction of Miss Compton-Burnett among highly civilised writers that her violence is always entirely credible.*

Violent action shakes up the characters in a novel, and it is foolish of writers to despise the strong situation: it may be most revealing about human behaviour. Mr Forster says, with some justice, that in the domain of violent physical action Jane Austen is

---

* The present writer must admit some difficulty in accepting the fraud in *Parents and Children*.

feeble and ladylike. Miss Compton-Burnett is neither: she comes serenely to violence like the great tragic artist that she is. She has so effectively prepared the way for it that when it inevitably comes, like war after a crisis, it is immediately felt to be a clearing of the air. The crime or adultery is seen to be less shocking than the daily cruelty at the breakfast-table. After the violence has died down, the chief characters, completely revealed, and to some extent participating in the purge by pity and terror, which has been the lot of readers and minor characters alike, resume their old life rather more quietly, and everything is hushed up, though everyone knows.

The violent happenings are of two sorts, as in Greek tragedy: either there is a crime, or the discovery of something dreadful in the past. These respectable families, descendants it might be of Jane Austen's Bennets, Bertrams or Knightleys, have within them the same seeds of destruction as the houses of Oedipus or of Agamemnon. Those happenings in that setting produce the effect which Miss Elizabeth Bowen has well described as 'sinister cosiness'.

If we read the *faits divers* in the newspapers we are apt to find unexplained and mysterious happenings: sometimes we meet with them in our own circle of acquaintance. A devoted husband and wife suddenly separate; a brilliant boy is found hanging in his bedroom. We do not know why, but there are some people who know, and who will take care that we never know. How many more must be the happenings we know nothing of at all. 'I think there are signs that strange things happen, though they do not emerge', says Miss Compton-Burnett. 'I believe it would go ill with many of us, if we were faced by a strong temptation, and I suspect that with some of us it does go ill.'

She shows us how strange things happen—she really shows us how. She traces them from their roots in the characters of the people to whom they happen. Therefore there is no vulgar melodrama, no matter how sensational the happenings are.

In *Pastors and Masters*, a mainly humorous study, the crime is only a fairly harmless literary forgery. In *Brothers and Sisters* it is found that Sophia Stace's husband was also her half-brother; and the secret of Christian Stace's parentage has caused other tangled relationships, which nearly become incestuous. The source of inspiration is again acknowledged. One of the characters remarks: 'We are beginning to leave off feeling branded, but all our friends seem shy of us. It is too like an ancient tragedy for them.'

In *Men and Wives*, Matthew Haslam poisons his domineering mother. In *More Women than Men*, Josephine is morally, though not legally, guilty of her nephew's wife's death. In *A House and Its Head*, Grant Edgeworth commits adultery with his uncle's second wife; their child is acknowledged as Duncan Edgeworth's son and heir, and is murdered by a servant at the instance of Sibyl, Grant's wife and Duncan's daughter, in order to remove the bar to Grant's inheritance of the family estate. In *Daughters and Sons* the crime is no more than a pretended (perhaps really attempted) suicide by Hetta Ponsonby. There is no crime or guilty secret in *A Family and a Fortune*, though two characters are driven to leave their homes sensationally in a snow-storm. Fraud of one sort or another is practised in *Parents and Children* and *Elders and Betters*: in the former it is dramatically unmasked, in the latter it remains triumphant—moreover the niece who has burnt one aunt's will drives another aunt to suicide.

The connection between tyranny and violence is generally causal. In *Men and Wives* the tyrant is the direct victim of the crime; in *More Women than Men* and *Daughters and Sons* a tyrant, in the danger of losing power, commits the crime in an attempt to preserve her domination. In *A House and Its Head* the tense family atmosphere, caused by Duncan's tyranny, is itself the cause of Sibyl's lack of mental balance, and of her crime. In the last two books the causation is less immediate—but it is the tyranny of Sir Jesse Sullivan that encourages Ridley Cranmer to think that his daughter-in-law will do anything to get out of his house, even to the point of assenting to a bigamous marriage—and the tyranny of Sukey Donne makes possible Anna's fraudulent substitution of a will in which she disinherits those who have the first claim on her.

It is the mark of bad, stupid or insincere characters that they are wholly or partly on the tyrant's side, through weakness, cowardice, hope of personal profit, or through a conventional or sentimental veneration of the Family as an institution, and of the tyrant as the obvious head of a family. Harriet Haslam is toadied by her lawyer, Dominic Spong, and Sabine and Hetta Ponsonby by their clergyman, Dr Chaucer. Most of the neighbours respect and over-indulge Duncan Edgeworth. It is only singularly acute people who avoid being taken in by Josephine Napier. The bad characters see virtues in the tyrants which have no objective existence; they do not dare to believe in the evil that is there, because they are too morally cowardly to take sides against it.

By contrast, and in themselves, the good characters are very good indeed. Where other novelists are often weak, Miss Compton-Burnett is strong, in the creation of likeable good characters. Her good people are intelligent and nice. They always have those qualities that we really most wish to find in our friends. Not that they are always conventionally irreproachable, though there is nothing to be said against Cassandra Jekyll in *A House and Its Head*, Helen Keats in *More Women than Men*, or several others. 'I like good people', says Maria Sloane in *A Family and a Fortune*. 'I never think people realise how well they compare with the others.'

The sex-life of Maria Rosetti, Felix Bacon and Grant Edgeworth has not been unblemished; Andrew, Dinah and Robin Stace, Evelyn Seymour, Terence Calderon and Dudley Gaveston are entirely idle; few of the good characters are particularly brave, most of them are irreligious, none of them are at all public-spirited —certainly they are not perfect. But they are serious, honest and sensitive, their human values are always right, and they will, if necessary, defend them. They never talk in slang or clichés; they never tell lies to others or to themselves about their feelings or motives—the bad characters think them unfeeling and selfish because they scorn pretence. They have virtues that are rare and unconventional: while many of the bad characters pride themselves on speaking good of everyone, the good characters know that it may be a higher form of charity to abuse tyrants to their victims, or to allow the victims the rare indulgence of speaking against their tyrants. The personal relations, whether of friendship or marriage or family affection, that subsist between the good characters, are as good as such relations can ever be, in life or in fiction. They are for Miss Compton-Burnett, as for Mr Forster, the supreme value—and she vindicates them against worse dangers than anyone in his novels has to face. Her arms, however, are not mystical; it is by truth, affection and intelligence only that her good characters conquer—and the greatest of these is intelligence. No one in fact or fiction has, or deserves to have, more self-respect than they. 'He respects us,' says a woman in *Parents and Children* about the old tyrant Sir Jesse. 'Ah, how I respect us!' replies her brother.

In consequence of their character the utterances of the good people have a directness and ruthlessness with which no mere cynic could compete.

'Let us all speak with a lack of decent feeling,' says Dinah Stace. 'It is time we did something out of keeping with the dignity of bereavement. It is a bad kind of dignity.'

'Other people's troubles are what they deserve. Ah, how they deserve them!' says Oscar Jekyll.

'Are you of the stuff that martyrs are made of?' says Chilton Ponsonby to his sister France, who is in danger of submitting to parental tyranny. 'I hope not; it is useless stuff.'

'I suppose I shall subscribe to hospitals,' says Dudley Gaveston, on coming into his fortune. 'That is how people seem to give to the poor. I suppose the poor are always sick. They would be, if you think. I once went round the cottages with Edgar, and I was too sensitive to go a second time. Yes, I was too sensitive even to set my eyes on the things which other people actually suffered, and I maintain that that was very sensitive.'

'Self-knowledge speaks ill for people,' says Hope Cranmer. 'It shows they are what they are almost on purpose.'

'I feel that to know all is to forgive all,' says Terence Calderon, 'and other people seem to forgive nothing. And no one can say they don't know all. I have never thought of any way of keeping it from them.'

Nor are the tyrants themselves incapable of goodness. Some of them are even capable of acts of almost heroic virtue, following hard upon others of extreme baseness. Sophia Stace, Josephine Napier and Matilda Seaton, the most intelligent of them, have moments of inspired sympathy. Where angels might fear to tread, and where the *anima naturaliter Christiana*, if a simple soul, would be likely to blunder, they walk sure-footed. It is a truism that a good heart may often guide a poor head: they prove that the converse may also be true. In them a fine understanding can produce fine and generous behaviour; in certain subtle difficulties it would be to them that one would turn for support, sooner than to many better-hearted people. Their creator reminds us that Wisdom is, after all, an intellectual virtue, and that the children of this world can be wiser (and, so far, to be more commended) than the children of light.

Most of the tyrants receive and deserve some respect and affection, even from their victims: the tyranny never quite abolishes family feeling, and when a tyrant has a bad fall the victims are chivalrously ready to pick him up. Some of them secure friendship and deep affection from characters of complete integrity, who see their faults clearly, but are yet fond of them—and this friendship and affection is also at least in part deserved. The tyrants are never all bad; and therefore untragic. Their fate cannot be a matter of indifference; in the one instance of tyrannicide, in *Men and Wives*, the pity of Harriet's death is as moving as the horror of Matthew's crime.

The last scene between Matthew and his mother can hardly have been read by those who profess to find neither action nor passion in Miss Compton-Burnett's books. It is wonderfully eloquent, and shows that she has the distinction, unique among living English prose-writers, of being capable of tragedy.

Matthew followed his mother upstairs, and was drawn by her into her room. 'Matthew,' she said, standing with her hand on his shoulder and her eyes looking up into his face, 'I want you to do something for me; not a great thing, dear; I would not ask that. I don't ask you to give up your work, or to give up your marriage; I know you cannot give up. I don't mean that any of us can; I am not saying anything to hurt. I only mean that I would not ask much of you. I just want you to put off your marriage for a few months, for your mother's sake, that she may have a little space of light before the clouds gather. I don't mean that my illness is coming again; I don't think it will come yet. And if it were, I would not use that to persuade you. I would not do what is not fair, while I am myself. I think you know I would not then. But I ask you simply, and as myself, to do this thing for me. I feel I can ask you, because I have seen your eyes on me tonight, and I have said to myself: "My son does not love me, not my eldest son. And it is my fault, because mothers can easily be loved by their sons. So I can ask this from him, because I cannot lose his love, or lessen it. I have not put it in him." And so I ask it of you, my dear.'

'Mother, what a way to talk!' said Matthew. 'Indeed your illness is not coming again. You could not be more at the height of your powers. Your speech was worth taking down. You may use it again. It was only I who heard it. My eyes show all this to you, when all my eyes are for Camilla at the moment, and if anyone knows that, it is you! I might tell you what your eyes show to me, and you would not have an answer. Now take one of your sleeping-tablets; I think I should take two; I have put them out on this table. And the marriage shall not happen until you sanction it. Camilla can get what she wants from this family, from you. She will have you as a friend before me as a husband. I daresay that will be the end.'

Harriet stood with her eyes searching her son's.

He kissed her and left her, and turned from the door and gave her the smile that should safeguard for both of them this memory.

It is not surprising that the only successful, living writer of English verse tragedy should show signs of Miss Compton-Burnett's influence both on the situation and the dialogue of *The Family Reunion*—though its action is more diffuse and less tragic than the greater moments in her novels. Perhaps it is not entirely fanciful to see Mr Eliot acknowledging this influence when he names one of his characters Ivy, and gives another an invitation to stay at 'Compton-Smith's place in Dorset'.

The tragic aspects of Miss Compton-Burnett's work have been dwelt on at this length, because of their immense significance. They mark her divergence from Jane Austen, and her unique position and stature as a novelist, and they indicate the importance which she attaches to her implied view of life. Briefly, she holds with Mr Forster that, to be good, people must be serious and truthful, and had better be intelligent; but she differs from him in adding that Charity begins at home. Her good and intelligent characters are not public-spirited, and her philanthropists are

D

almost invariably prigs or bores, though delightfully entertaining.

Lydia Fletcher in *Pastors and Masters* has her men's class, her
'dear men things'. In *Men and Wives* there is an inimitable working
party. The village in *A House and Its Head* is cursed with three
women, ruthlessly going about doing good to their neighbours.

For, like Miss Austen, Miss Compton-Burnett is a great comic
writer.

'I am such a votary of the comic muse. "No," I have said, when
people have challenged me, "I will not have comedy pushed into a
back place." I think tragedy and comedy are a greater, wider
thing than tragedy by itself. And comedy is so often seen to have
tragedy behind it.'

This is true of her work, though it is an absurd character who
says it. As well as humorously exploiting situations, and making
use of epigrammatic brilliance in dialogue, she is a great creator of
comic characters. Many of them play an active part as the philan-
thropic busybodies or the tyrant's parasites, to whom reference has
been made—roles which are often combined. Others, like Mrs
Christy who has just been quoted, have a more simply decorative
function.

A scene from *Pastors and Masters* illustrates the simpler form of
humour, rare in her later work, of several absurd characters in
action together.

'Mrs Merry,' Miss Basden said, in a rather high monotone, 'the
boys are saying that the marmalade is watery. I am telling them that
no water is used in marmalade, that marmalade does not contain
water, so I do not see how it can be.'

'I do not see how it can be, either; but of course I wish to be told
if anything is not as nice as it can be. Let me taste the marmalade.'

Miss Basden offered a spoon from the pot.

'It seems to me that is very nice. Perhaps I am not a judge of
marmalade. I do not care to eat it on bread with butter myself. One
or the other is enough for me. But it seems to be very nice.'

'Mother, don't water the boys' preserves,' said Mr Merry, nodding
his head up and down. 'Don't try to make things go further than
they will go, you know. The game isn't worth the candle.'

'I do not understand you, dear. There is never any extra water in
preserves. They would not keep if they had water in them. There

would not be any object in it. It would be less economical not more.'

'Oh, well, Mother, I don't know anything about the kitchen business and that. But if the marmalade is not right, let us have it right another time. That is all I mean.'

'I do not think you know what you mean, dear.'

'No, Mother, no; very likely I don't.'

'The housekeeping is not your province, Mr Merry,' said Miss Basden. 'You will have us coming and telling you how to teach Latin, if you are not careful.'

'Ah, Miss Basden, ah, you saucy lady!'

A source of amusement is the invariable curiosity of the minor characters about the central tragedy; this is dissembled by the dishonest, and frankly acknowledged by the more worthy.

'Our curiosity is neither morbid nor ordinary. It is the kind known as devouring.' (Evelyn Seymour, in *Daughters and Sons*.)

'We can't put gossip off until we return from London. It has a frail hold on life like all precious things.' (Julian Wake, in *Brothers and Sisters*.)

'I don't like things to pass me by, without my hearing about them. We are meant to be interested in what the Almighty ordains.' (Sarah Middleton, in *A Family and a Fortune*.)

The brilliance and wit of the dialogue have increased with each successive book. Even in the more conventional and easily detachable epigrams there are turns and rhythms which unmistakably show their author: 'Saying a thing of yourself does not mean that you like to hear other people say it. And they do say it differently.'

'Being cruel to be kind is just ordinary cruelty with an excuse made for it. And it is right that it should be more resented, as it is.'

The extraordinarily subtle humour of her finer writing would need illustration by a long, sustained passage, though it is suggested by such a passage as this from *More Women than Men*, where Felix Bacon is talking to Josephine Napier about the staff of her school.

'I hope they none of them presume upon their friendship?'

'I trust that they deal with me fully as a friend. I hardly understand that phrase, "presume upon friendship".'

'I quite understand it. Shall we have a gossip about your staff?'

'No!' said Josephine. 'When you have known me a little longer, you will know that my mistresses, in their presence and in their absence are safe with me. I hope I could say that about all my friends.'

'I hoped you could not. But it is interesting that they would not be safe if we had the gossip. They must have treated you fully as a friend. I almost feel we have had it.'

It is not to be supposed that the characters in Miss Compton-Burnett's novels are only types, because they are easily classifiable. They are in fact very subtly differentiated. They are limited on the whole to certain broad categories, because the plot is to deal with certain kinds of happenings. Since the happenings come out of the people, that entails certain kinds of people. Happenings cannot come out of types, they must come out of real characters. The twelve tyrants, for example, all stand out distinct in the memory: though similarity of situation may sometimes cause them to speak alike, one could in nearly every case pick out the speech of one from that of all the others.

Critics who are unwilling to take the trouble that this very difficult writer requires, or who are not sensitive to subtleties of speech, complain that all her people talk alike. She herself has written in the *Conversation*: 'However differently characters are conceived—and I have never conceived two in the same way—they tend to give a similar impression, if they are people of the same kind, produced by the same mind, and carried out by the same hand, and possibly one that is acquiring a habit.'

Each of her characters talks like the others in the sense that they all talk with maximum clarity and self-revelation, and in a polished bookish speech—in this they are all more alike than they are like any character by any other writer. But they have all been conceived with such clarity that with patience they are easily distinguishable. Moreover two practices of the author's which make her characters superficially more alike, in fact mark their difference. When one character tries to imitate another, who is a more brilliant conversationalist, we are at once aware of the imitation—this could not be the case unless both characters were very distinct in our minds. (Thus in *Brothers and Sisters*, Latimer imitates Julian; in *Men and Wives*, Kate imitates Rachel Hardisty.)

Her second device occurs in her later novels, and is an even greater *tour de force*. She brings out family resemblances, so that in *A Family and a Fortune*, the little boy, Aubrey, combines something of the peevishness of his maternal grandfather, Oliver Seaton, with more of the clear-headed fineness of his paternal uncle, Dudley Gaveston (whose manner of speech he also consciously imitates). Nevertheless all three characters remain entirely distinct in the reader's imagination, and Aubrey is one of the most moving child characters in fiction. This sort of achievement is perhaps unique—it is much more than mere technical virtuosity, it is real character creation.

Her treatment of children is particularly admirable. Children in fiction have been more sentimentalised, lied about and betrayed than any other class of being. The more intelligent the writer, the better he treats them. Henry James and Proust have written better about them than anyone. An author so unsentimental and intelligent as Miss Compton-Burnett might be expected either to leave them alone, or to deal with them perfectly, as she has done. Although her narrative takes place almost exclusively in the form of very highly developed conversation among remarkably articulate people, she has all the same managed to draw shy and even very young children brilliantly—and she knows, what most people forget, how extremely early the character is distinct. Nevill Sullivan in *Parents and Children* is only three, and a very definite character, with his own kind of independence and protective cunning.

There are few more triumphant revelations of the child mind in English literature than in the scenes in *Elders and Betters* where Julius and Dora Calderon practise their extraordinary private religion. Their prayer to their God, after the death of their aunt and the suicide of their mother is often quoted.

'O great and good and powerful god, Chung, grant that our life may not remain clouded, as it is at this present. And grant that someone may guide us in the manner of our mother, so that we may not wander without direction in the maze of life. For although we would have freedom, if it be thy will, yet would we be worthy of being our mother's children. And if there is danger of our inheriting the weaknesses of our mother and our aunt, thy late handmaids, guard us from them, O god, and grant that we may live to a ripe old age. For it would not be worth while to suffer the trials of childhood, if they were not to lead to fullness of days. And we pray thee to comfort our father and our brother and sister; and if they are in less need of comfort than beseems them, pardon them, O god, and lead them to know the elevation of true grief.'

Miss Compton-Burnett's novels are certainly of permanent value, though they may never be 'popular classics'. Her work continues to become increasingly attractive to serious students of literature. Many will find her style rebarbative on a first approach: all must find it difficult. Only repeated re-reading can extract all the treasure from her finest work; and it is hard to persuade people to give the attention to a major novelist that they are ready to squander on minor poetry. It does not seem too much, or nearly enough, to claim for her that, of all English novelists now writing she is the greatest and the most original artist.

Appendix III, from *A Treatise on the Novel*, 1947.

Edward Sackville-West

LADIES WHOSE BRIGHT PENS . . .

IT MIGHT BE thought that Miss Elizabeth Bowen and Miss Ivy Compton-Burnett were writers too dissimilar to be brought together in a single essay. It is true that a close comparison of their methods and achievements could scarcely fail to be unfair to both of them. But I hope to show that there are points of resemblance, as well as of contrast, which make it worth while to consider them together.

That both are women is already important. Disagreeing with Dr Johnson's low opinion of feminine ability, I find that when women take the trouble to form a literary style it tends to be a sharper and more flexible instrument than most men command. Gifted with rapidity, the female intelligence is far less given to pedantry and sententiousness. Its characteristic weapons are the adroit phrase, the cunning sentence, the startling yet homely image, the eye which pierces to the heart of a complex personal relationship, and a refreshing freedom from those political obsessions which nag and distort the visions of men. And for kindred reasons women writers seem on the whole more careful than we to keep within their scope. Nowadays it is a common occurrence to find male novelists describing milieux which they have obviously never even visited, simply because they fear the critics' parrot cry: "Mr So-and-So leaves too much out of his picture." If the picture is properly composed and true to its subject, it is complete: what is omitted is strictly irrelevant. Only the Marxian bigot despises Jane Austen for writing of what she knew and ignoring certain aspects of her times (and she ignores less than appears on the surface). Both Miss Bowen and Miss Compton-Burnett know their limitations; and knowing them means turning them to account. Miss Bowen marches with the times in the sense that the scenes of her stories are roughly contemporaneous with their publication; while Miss Compton-Burnett's world is the comparatively distant and static one of the late Victorian days. At the same time it should be noticed that both novelists exhaust their material; there are no loose ends; their books are sonatas of which the subjects are very thoroughly explored. Fascinated, like all considerable artists, by the richness and profundity of a single subject, they concentrate all their powers on the gradual unravelment— volume by volume—of the situation to which their temperaments have given them the key. And a precise consciousness of their scope dictates the unit of composition: in Miss Bowen's case the individual trembling on the verge of irreconcilable ties; in Miss Compton-Burnett's, the family.

*   *   *

The family. . . . The disintegrating effect of two wars has tended to drive novelists away from the direct treatment of this subject. For Miss Compton-Burnett it is not only the source of her ideas—and therefore of her plots—but also the focus of all other relationships. Her characters are in the first place (as the titles of her novels imply) sons, daughters, wives, brothers, etc., and only in the second place separate individuals with lives of their own. Like the Greek dramatists, with whom she has sometimes been compared, Miss Compton-Burnett finds in the family the central meeting-place of love and hate; so that in the working out of her books tragedy takes the form of a tightening of the family tie, comedy that of a loosening of the same tie, when those who have enough courage escape into the world. (We never follow them into that world, the advantages of which are taken for granted.) In a scrap of dialogue worth quoting for other characteristic features, Miss Compton-Burnett implies her view of this situation:

> 'What is a little impatience, hastiness—tyranny, if it must be said— compared with a real isolation and loneliness?'
> 'I am afraid it must be said, and they are a great deal worse.'

Two more quotations should serve to explain the richness and fascination of the subject to which this novelist devotes her astonishing powers. The first is from the same book (*Daughters and Sons*).

'What I can't understand about that family,' said Rowland, 'is how they say what they like all the time, and yet seem to be afraid. Can anyone explain it?'

'No one yet,' said Miss Marcon. 'Alfred may be able to presently. But families can seldom be explained, and they make better gossip without any explanation. To know all is to forgive all, and that would spoil everything.'

In the end of these novels we *do* know all, and forgive all, and everything *is* spoilt, in the sense that nothing—absolutely nothing —further remains to be said. The material is exhausted and our satisfaction with the work of art is complete.

My third quotation is from a later book, *Parents and Children*: 'You should not want to know the things in people's minds. If you were meant to hear them, they would be said.' So much is in fact said in these novels, which are nine-tenths dialogue, that the suppressed idea or emotion assumes the importance that in other novelists requires a whole scene, or sequence of scenes, to build up. One of the advantages of Miss Compton-Burnett's exquisite conversation is that any direct statement of feeling or intention has the force of a violent gesture. The 'cast' is always assembled in such a way that there is one character, and one only, who by making such statements carries the plot a step forward. Like flying bombs, these stories proceed by jet propulsion, and the explosion, when at last it occurs, hits those who were least prepared for it.

A society, the members of which are so highly conscious of their interdependence, creates its own destiny; and the flying bomb becomes a boomerang. If they could, they would leave stones unturned; but their circumstances make this impossible. To them, all life is one long process of more or less painful discovery. 'When people shut themselves up they cease to separate occasions'; and—with equal inevitability—they become like actors intoxicated by their own eloquence, wit, self-pity and self-love. Indeed, the degree of articulateness displayed by everyone— from servants and children to the tyrant of the household (an invariable figure)—seems alleged, until it is realised that this is a stylistic convention such as every artist has the right to adopt.

That everyone in these novels employs the same tone and the
same large and scholarly vocabulary does not, strangely enough,
impair the vigour of the characterisation, except in a few instances
where the dimness of the outline is due to other causes as well.
Indeed, Miss Compton-Burnett's signal triumph in this field
seems to me quite sufficient to justify repudiation of the modern
insistence on naturalistic dialogue. In *Manservant and Maidservant*,
for example—a story in which the convention is carried to its
furthest extreme—the characters whose idiom is least natural
are precisely those who emerge as most real and pathetic. I am
thinking of George, the footman, Miss Buchanan, the keeper of
the village shop, and at least three of the children (Marcus,
Jasper and Avery). Their characters emerge in what they say—
not in their manner of saying it—and, still more perhaps, from
the occasions they choose for displaying loss of patience in a
short, stinging sentence.

*   *   *

It need not be supposed that this remarkable invention owes
nothing to former novelists; but those who seek its origin in an
obvious place (e.g. in Henry James) will return empty-handed.
The true hiding-place, I suggest, is perhaps rather an unexpected
one. No one would be surprised to discover a resemblance
between the Compton-Burnett milieu and that of *Cranford*;
but in a finer, lesser-known novel by Mrs Gaskell—*Wives and
Daughters*—another kind of resemblance is too startling to be
accidental. I quote, for example, the scene in which Cynthia
Kirkpatrick and her half-sister, Molly Gibson, are discussing the
local grandees, Lord and Lady Cumnor, with Osborne, the
elder son of Squire Hamley.

'Are the family coming to the Towers this autumn?'
'I believe so. But I don't know, and I don't much care. They don't
take kindly to me,' continued Cynthia, 'and so I suppose I'm not
generous enough to take kindly to them.'
'I should have thought that such a very unusual blot in their
discrimination would have interested you in them as extraordinary
people,' said Osborne, with a little air of conscious gallantry.
'Isn't that a compliment?' said Cynthia, after a pause of mock

meditation. 'If anyone pays me a compliment, please let it be short and clear! I'm very stupid at finding out hidden meanings.'

'Then such speeches as "you are very pretty", or "you have charming manners", are what you prefer. Now, I pique myself on wrapping up my sugar-plums delicately.'

'Then would you please to write them down, and at my leisure I'll parse them.'

'No! It would be too much trouble. I'll meet you half-way, and study clearness next time.'

'What are you two talking about?' said Molly, resting on her light spade.

'It's only a discussion on the best way of administering compli-ments,' said Cynthia, taking up her flower-basket again, but not going out of reach of the conversation.

'I don't like them at all in any way,' said Molly. 'But perhaps, it's rather sour grapes with me,' she added.

'Nonsense!' said Osborne. 'Shall I tell you what I heard of you at the ball?'

'Or shall I provoke Mr Preston,' said Cynthia, 'to begin upon you? It's like turning a tap, such a stream of pretty speeches flows out at the moment.' Her lips curled with scorn.

'For you, perhaps,' said Molly; 'but not for me.'

'For any woman. It's his notion of making himself agreeable. If you dare me, Molly, I'll try the experiment, and you'll see with what success.'

'No! don't, pray!' said Molly in a hurry. 'I do so dislike him!'

'Why?' said Osborne, roused to a little curiosity by her vehem-ence.

'Oh! I don't know. He never seems to know what one is feeling.'

'He wouldn't care, if he did know,' said Cynthia. 'And he might know he is not wanted.'

'If he chooses to stay, he cares little whether he is wanted or not.'

'Come, this is very interesting,' said Osborne. 'It is like the strophe and anti-strophe in a Greek chorus. Pray, go on.'

Osborne takes the words out of our mouth: they are an oblique tribute to the patness of the dialogue Mrs Gaskell always had it in her to write.

Further on in the same book occurs another and shorter passage, which I cannot resist quoting, for it is even closer to the style of Miss Compton-Burnett. Cynthia and Molly are discussing with

Mrs Gibson the illness of Osborne Hamley and his brother Roger's chances of succeeding to the property—a Compton-Burnett situation, if ever there was one.

> 'Why, my dear, it is a very natural thought. For poor Roger's sake, you know, one wishes it not to be so very very long an engagement; and I was only answering Molly's question, after all. One can't help following out one's thoughts. People must die, you know—young, as well as old.'
> 'If I ever suspected Roger of following out his thoughts in a similar way,' said Cynthia, 'I'd never speak to him again.'
> 'As if he would!' said Molly, warm in her turn. 'You know he never would; and you shouldn't suppose it of him, Cynthia—no, not even for a moment!'
> 'I can't see the great harm of it all, for my part,' said Mrs Gibson plaintively. 'A young man strikes us all as looking very ill—and I'm sure I'm sorry for it; but illness very often leads to death. Surely you agree with me there, and what's the harm of saying so? Then Molly asks what will happen, if he dies; and I try to answer her question. I don't like talking or thinking of death any more than anyone else; but I should think myself wanting in strength of mind, if I could not look forward to the consequences of death. I really think we're commanded to do so, somewhere in the Bible or the Prayer Book.'
> 'Do you look forward to the consequences of my death, Mamma?' asked Cynthia.

It must be admitted that Miss Compton-Burnett's people have a good deal more to talk about than Mrs Gaskell's. Murder, incest, suicide, theft, immolation, relentless mental cruelty, self-martyrdom, forgery, burning of legal papers: the worst of which human nature is capable is examined on the level of a solecism, between the dropping of a teacup and the entrance of a parlour-maid to collect the fragments. Apart from physical violence and starvation, there is no feature of the totalitarian regime which has not its counterpart in the atrocious families depicted in these books. That this is not immediately obvious is due partly to the Cranfordian background—the quiet, dignified, medium-sized country house standing in what Lady Catherine de Bourgh would have described as a 'small' park, with its village, its rector, its doctor, its retired couple living on savings or a

'genteel sufficiency'. These people live too intensely to have time
for enjoying their material world. If anything, the roses round the
door make them love mother less—and she is seldom lovable,
in any case. Money is always important to them, but only in so
far as it affects their relationships. They are mildly snobbish. Their
sense of social responsibility is implicit, and if lacking is remarked
on. Perfect urbanity is the first rule of their intercourse. In these
embowered, rook-enchanted concentration camps (the landscape
is evoked, hardly ever described) the horrors are made acceptable,
but not blunted, by Politeness and Wit. That is, after all, what
manners are for; without them, men and women are incomplete.
Self-control is rarely lost in these novels, but where it is lost the
result is proportionately upsetting to everyone, the reader
included. Anger, despair, exasperation, increase the loftiness of
the speech, so that the characters seem to exult in the eloquence
of their feelings. Thus, in *Brothers and Sisters*, Dinah Stace, ex-
ceeded by grief and by her mother Sophia's demands upon her
forbearance, speaks her mind to the housekeeper whose clumsy
inquisitiveness has revealed the family skeleton:

> 'Oh, well, Patty, if people will listen at doors, we are helpless. . . .
> We can't allow for that; though it does seem the rule of the house.
> And we have to talk to Sophia about it. She can't keep it off her
> mind. How is she to make an effort now, for the first time in her
> life? If people will leave no stone unturned, to find out what they
> ought not to know, they must go on turning stones. There are some
> more to turn. Sophia must be served until the end.'

Here exhaustion induced by strong feeling is evident, but so is
the control, which is apparent in the short, measured phrases,
and the moderation of the words. But when, as seldom happens,
Miss Compton-Burnett decides that the moment is appropriate
for somebody to lose his or her head, the tempo changes. In
the following speech, taken from the end of *Daughters and Sons*,
the author shows what she can achieve by directness:

> John gave his sister a look and turned away, and she suddenly rose
> and spoke in a harsh, stumbling voice, in tense, stumbling sentences,
> which seemed to be torn from some depth within her below the
> level of speech.

'So Edith is everything, is she? Edith, whom you married because you thought she had given you money and would give you more! Edith, whom you married for the paltry sums you thought she would earn and go on giving you! You did not want her for herself! You did not want to earn for your wife! She was to earn for you. And the plan was an empty one after all. It is France who earned the money, France who gave it to you, France who wrote the book that won it! She hid behind Edith's name, because you were jealous of her. Jealous of your daughter! She had to hide because she was afraid of your jealousy! Oh, I know it; I know it all. I know how Mater thought she found out; I saw her tamper with the letters; I saw her read the one addressed to Edith, which was meant for France. I know when she told you; I know when you talked about it; I know how you told each other that Edith would have other money in the end. And Edith knows why you married her. She found it out and did not dare tell you. She did not dare tell her husband that for the time she had only herself to give! She was afraid of the power of your feelings. Oh, people are afraid of you, though you think they are only afraid of me. It is only of women that people are afraid. What a welter of deceit I have found in my family! What a moral mess I have stumbled on unawares, stumbled on because it was everywhere. First Mater must deceive us all; then she deceived you; then you deceived Edith. Now Edith has begun to deceive you, though I admit she was afraid. France had already deceived you, though I admit she was afraid. Think of the feeling she had for you, when she wanted to save you the humiliation of not being able to earn; and did not dare to face your jealousy, and so took refuge behind that letter from a stranger! She knew what you wanted; she knew you. And I know you now; I know you. I am not going to do anything more; I am not going to serve you. I am going to live for myself, as you do. You have taught me how to do it, and I have learned. You tell me you have learned the lessons I have taught, and I can tell you the same. It is Edith who will have to serve you, because she cannot work, cannot earn the petty sums that mean so much to you. They are so paltry, these sums of money that mould your life.'

In the finely managed arc of this torrential speech I seem to descry the pattern of Miss Compton-Burnett's literary heritage. Though the resemblances are in some ways misleading, her novels are conceived on the same moral and intellectual level as those of Henry James; behind both writers, at a distance which, because of their excellence, seems less great than it is, stand the vehement yet composed rhetoric of the Grand Siècle, and the later, more bitter knowledge of Laclos.

★   ★   ★

Miss Compton-Burnett's progress in her art has been more considerable than might appear, in view of the curious and no doubt deliberate uniformity of her novels. For, like a sculptor obsessed by the human figure, she recommences the same task in each successive book, and relies for variety on the endless combinations of spoken language. Her characters are comparatively few and reappear constantly under different names; but each incarnation reveals some new facet of experience. Her first book, *Dolores* (published in 1911), is indeed not very characteristic and is chiefly interesting for the few glimpses of her later style which it contains. A lachrymose, amateurish book, it occasionally startles one with things like this:

> 'How do you do, Mrs Cassell?' said Mrs Blackwood. 'We were all beginning to wonder if anything had prevented your coming.'
> 'How do you know we were, Mother? We have none of us said so,' said Elsa.

This foreshadows the portentous domestic tyrants of *Brothers and Sisters*, *A House and Its Head* and *Daughters and Sons*, as well as the disillusioned, completely intelligent, but dutiful children who suffer under them.

With *Pastors and Masters* (1925) the mature style is already formed in all essential features: it only remained for the artist to exploit the potentialities of so remarkable an invention. Her own view of the matter is set out, in modest but very illuminating fashion, in a dialogue with Miss M. Jourdain published in *Orion*. But to the present writer the effect of her art recalls the aims of the Cubist movement in painting, at its inception. Like a Picasso of 1913, a Compton-Burnett novel is not concerned with decoration or with observation of the merely contingent, nor is it interested in exhibiting the author's personality or in exploiting a romantic dream. It is constructive, ascetic, low in tone, classical. It enquires into the meanings—the syntactical force—of the things we all say, as the Cubist enquired into the significance of shapes and planes divorced from the incidence of light and the accidents of natural or utilitarian construction. These novels contain very few descriptive passages, and none where description is indulged in for its own sake, or for Impressionistic ends; and in this connection it is significant that Miss Compton-Burnett seems to scorn the aid of images. This does not, I think, strike us at the time of reading; it is not until we take up some other book that we realise to what extent nearly all novelists rely on metaphor and simile to enliven their scene.

I have described these novels as being nine-tenths dialogue, which gives the measure of the space Miss Compton-Burnett allows herself for noting the scene, the aspect and movement of persons, and any comment she may find necessary. All this is reduced to the absolute minimum and in its abrupt succinctness hardly amounts to more than what one expects to find in the stage directions of a play. The result is something unique, though it has affinities with the tradition of the dramatic legend which was instituted by Plato and includes Fontenelle, Diderot and W. S. Landor.

But it is her zeal for measuring the *temperature* of emotion— the graph described from moment to moment by the action of the plot on the alert sensibilities of her characters—which is responsible both for the continuously witty surface of her writing and the deeper truth of her picture. Like Henry James, Miss Compton-Burnett is much concerned to preserve an amusing surface, as well as a polite one; and this remains true of the tragic passages in her books. Indeed, in those which deal with the most frightful happenings (*Brothers and Sisters, Men and Wives, More Women than Men, A House and Its Head*) the comic relief is more pronounced and more evenly distributed than in the later novels, of which the plots are considerably less lurid. But it is her anxious attention to Truth which, more than anything else, gives to her books their quality of timeless relevance. Her wit has many sides, but it excludes absolutely the wise-crack, the smart epigram, the modish or private sally. 'People don't feel as much as you want them to.' This assumption is fundamental to all these novels: it is the arrow on the thermometer which marks 98·4°. And the

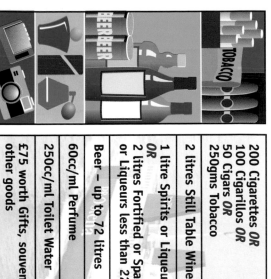

200 Cigarettes *OR*
100 Cigarillos *OR*
50 Cigars *OR*
250gms Tobacco

2 litres Still Table Wine

1 litre Spirits or Liqueurs over 22% Vol.
OR
2 litres Fortified or Sparkling Wine,
or Liqueurs less than 22% vol.

Beer – up to 72 litres

60cc/ml Perfume

250cc/ml Toilet Water

£75 worth Gifts, souvenirs and all
other goods

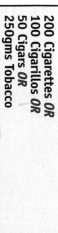

No person under 17 years of age may purchase alcohol or tobacco.

Since the 1st January 1993, under European Union regulations, **you can buy your whole duty-free limit on the outward crossing PLUS the same again on your return and bring back BOTH, provided they are for your personal use.**

In order to make your duty-free purchases, you must present this voucher in person to the cashier in the Duty-free Shop when you make a purchase. We regret that we cannot sell duty-free goods to you without this voucher or over the EU regulation limits.

This voucher shows your personal entitlement and is NOT transferable. It remains the property of P&O Stena Line Ltd.

A voucher will be isssued to you for each leg of the journey.

EU law sets out guidance levels for personal use and these levels include anything bought duty-free. You may be required to prove, if asked, that any goods you have which exceed these limits are not for commercial purposes. For further information see Customs Notice 1 or ask at the information office.

A 166771

P&O Stena

movement of the book is the to-and-fro rhythm of a tug-of-war between those who do not wish to feel too much and those who are determined to make them feel more than they can bear—until the rope breaks.

I do not want to give the impression that I consider these novels faultless. In common with other important artists Miss Compton-Burnett has a number of failings which are perhaps inherent in her very personal idiom. They are easily described:

(1) She tends to fill her canvas too rapidly, and this mistake is aggravated by the perfunctory way in which she describes her characters, so that we are in constant danger of forgetting or confusing them. It must, however, be pointed out that in her later novels this fault is less apparent.

(2) She cannot manage masculine men. Her males are either overtly effete (e.g. Alfred Marcon in *Daughters and Sons*), or possessed by a feline power-mania (e.g. Duncan Edgeworth in *A House and Its Head*).

(3) Her plots are not easily remembered in detail, or distinguished one from another. This is not a serious charge, for her emphasis lies elsewhere; but it argues a certain rigidity of imagination and probably has some connection with

(4) Her subsidiary characters are often (but by no means always) too 'flat'. Even regarded as a chorus, they are too dim in outline and tend, moreover, to be always of the same type.

(5) Her chief characters do not develop in the course of the book, they only loom larger or dwindle, according as the author lengthens or shortens her opera-glass.

(6) When Action supervenes, she skates over it as quickly as possible, in the manner of Jane Austen. At such moments a kind of deadly calm descends on the page; which is in a way effective, but tends to spoil what in music is called the balance of parts.

These faults, although they add up to something, do not seriously affect the brilliance and gravity of these amazing books, or the intense satisfaction that arises from submitting oneself to Miss Compton-Burnett's regime. If her novels are tiring to read, that is because the non-stop rallies, the wonderful patness, the immense logical sequences, make it difficult to decide where to put the book down, when it becomes necessary to attend to something else. Once launched on the stream one must attend completely to every word, until the end is reached. But although these difficulties render her work no light undertaking for the reader, the reward is proportionate—not only in the illumination of so much in life that other, and perhaps more scopious, novelists agree to ignore, but in irresistible laughter. For these books are, one and all, monumentally funny.

*   *   *

Cleverness, with which the great Victorians were so liberally gifted and which, in all centuries until the present, was accepted as the nervous system of the intellect, has fallen into disrepute in England (but not, however, elsewhere in the British Isles). This distrust of nimble-mindedness has naturally accompanied the decline in elegance and quality, and the admiration for mediocrity, which are the inevitable outcome of an unjustified belief in 'natural' equality. In public life this tendency led to preferring Mr Baldwin to Lord Curzon—a course the results of which many people now agree to deplore; while in matters of art it is perhaps not surprising that a public which cannot respect Bartok, Hindemith and Picasso should find it easier to applaud John Ireland, E. J. Moeran and Stanley Spencer. Where literature is concerned the distinction is not so clear; but it remains true that to call a novelist clever is tantamount to accusing him or her of superficiality or of underhand appeal to a reactionary minority.

Both Miss Elizabeth Bowen and Miss Compton-Burnett are extremely clever, though in different ways. The latter, as I hope I have conveyed, enjoys a special ability akin to that of a logician or a statist; and the beauty of her books arises from the harmony and symmetry of a carefully constructed world. Miss Bowen, on the other hand, is clever in the generally accepted sense of the word: her style, at once smooth and sparkling, is constantly tasselled with fresh and startlingly apt images; in narrative she is mistress of the oblique and suggestive; her dialogue is economical but highly characterised; her plots (described by herself as 'the knowing of destination') are sufficiently ingenious and perfectly adapted to the idea; and she is supremely sensitive to the poetic moment. As her 'Notes on Writing a Novel' show, she is as highly conscious an artist as Miss Compton-Burnett; but the reader who is uninterested in technique will be less aware of this fact, while reading one of Miss Bowen's novels or stories, because her method of rendering life is not (as painters say) pushed nearly so far. She stands in the same relation to Miss Compton-Burnett as Vuillard stands to Braque, or Sickert to Ben Nicholson.

Miss Bowen's scope of reference has a wider variety than Miss Compton-Burnett's, but whatever she writes of she knows. It is the same world—that of highly educated, civilised people— but altered and extended by the general loosening up and over-lapping that have taken place in the last thirty years. A single sentence from one of Miss Bowen's most recent stories nicely implies the point of view from which her comment originates:

'As you know, I was at Sandyhill yesterday: they are taking two more of cousin Rosanna's servants, so she has decided to close some more of the house, including that little ante-room through to the library.'

A less careful novelist would probably have written simply 'the library'; it is that little ante-room which shows, not only how completely Miss Bowen dominates her ambience, but her precise awareness of the visual situation offered, at all points, by her choice of scene. For, just as Miss Compton-Burnett is essentially an *ear*, Miss Bowen, despite the unquestionably real quality of her dialogue, is above all an *eye*. Her business is with the complexities of the heart, light with perceptive wonder or heavy with some burden of unwelcome knowledge. But it is always the visual accompaniment of emotion which gives to that emotion its force and colour, and so fixes it in our minds. The scene, however fleeting, is always *set*; the characters may not give voice to their thoughts, but a sudden sunbeam, a shape of cloud, a sly look, a door ajar, a smouldering cigarette—these speak for them.

Like Miss Compton-Burnett, then, Elizabeth Bowen exhausts her material, but in pursuit of a very different theme. This— to put it briefly—is the conflict between Innocence and Guilt (using those words in the Christian sense). It is the same theme which fascinated Henry James in so many stories, from *The American* to *The Wings of the Dove* and *The Golden Bowl*. I say 'conflict', but 'attraction' better describes this most poignant of all situations; and it is in the corruption of guileless persons by those who simultaneously love and hate them, that Miss Bowen finds her clue. Innocence is not the prerogative of girls, but although she has portrayed at least two innocent males (Colonel Bent in *The House in Paris*, Major Brutt in *The Death of the Heart*), it is natural that women should be her main target. Intense feeling —perhaps the most intense *personal* feeling he ever knew—kept Henry James at a respectful distance from Daisy Miller, from Milly Theale and Maggie Verver. Miss Bowen takes the analysis a step further, into the dead centre of the personality, exploring that distressful limbo which rings with the faint cries of those whose trust has been betrayed. She is adept at conveying to us the fateful calm in which, at the outset of her novels, the heroine waits for something to happen. And it is always the worst that happens—the humiliation that injures the soul so much more direly than physical rape.

> *Heiss mich nicht reden, heiss mich schweigen,*
> *Denn mein Geheimnis ist mir Pflicht:*
> *Ich möchte dir mein ganzes Innre zeigen,*
> *Allein das Schicksal will es nicht.*

Portia (*The Death of the Heart*), Emmeline (*To the North*), Lois (*The Last September*), Karen (*The House in Paris*): these fine-grained creatures—*jeunes filles en fleur* trembling on the brink of 'life'—are the descendants of Mignon, but for them fate (*das Schicksal*) is less foreseen. They all experience the heartbreak which is not (save in one instance) irreparable, either through the insouciance of philanderers (Portia, Emmeline, Karen), or through the selfish conventionality of their immediate surroundings (Lois). Evil, as a motive, has not in these novels the impersonal, terrifying power, working *from outside*, that it acquires in the work of François Mauriac or Graham Greene; but its precipitation in the alembic set a-boil by a chance encounter is the measure of Miss Bowen's seriousness as a critic of life, and of her importance in the history of English fiction. For it should be noticed that her most characteristic creations are distinctively English: one would not expect to find Portia or Emmeline or Lois in a Latin country, nor yet in the United States of today.

*   *   *

As if to defend the subtlety of her theme, Elizabeth Bowen's plots are usually simple and well-defined; unlike Miss Compton-Burnett's they are impossible to forget or to confuse one with another. Uninterested in complexity for its own sake, she never attempts a sub-plot, and the many subsidiary lives which surround the object of attention are never allowed to engage too much of the reader's interest. Nevertheless, the air in these books is easier to breathe than that of Miss Compton-Burnett's secret sessions. Miss Bowen enjoys a large cast: her people and places are open on all sides. There is a general air of busyness, of work in the background; light and space surround her characters, even in their tenser moments. These novels are full of movement, in the literal as well as the figurative sense, and this is perhaps why we never feel crowded out of the page—as we sometimes do in a novel by Miss Compton-Burnett.

Though true of all her novels, these assertions need to be modified in the case of what I consider Miss Bowen's finest achievements, *The Last September* and *The House in Paris*. The first of these is an idyll, and therefore more static than (for instance) *To the North*. The setting has some of Miss Compton-Burnett's enclosed quality. But the discursive style, light and quick as a dragonfly, dispels any sense of difficulty. Perhaps because this is an early book, a slight self-consciousness mars the surface; but the picture of an Anglo-Irish country-house, spell-bound in the lovely autumnal calm that precedes its extinction, could hardly be better done. The double tragedy, with which the book ends, completes the structure without weighing it down. Miss Bowen's debt to Jane Austen shows here (more clearly than in her first novel, *The Hotel*, which happens to be lighter in tone) in an uncommon ability to treat tragedy on the same level as comedy. This could not always be a suitable impression to produce; that she has chosen it here is an example of her cleverness in discerning the exact tone of feeling with which Lois, her uncle and aunt and her lover, will respond to events.

'People do not feel as much as you want them to.'

Miss Bowen would not agree to that, and in her most artistically successful—her most mysterious and poetic—novel, *The House in Paris*, she gives us the full range of her subtle imagination. In this extraordinary and very beautiful book the innocent and the guilty are less sharply distinguished than elsewhere in Miss Bowen's work, and the atmosphere is more sinister. Although there is plenty of movement the dark little house of Mme Fisher dominates the whole book and casts its ambiguous shadow across the Channel into the sunlit, spacious, everyday world of the Michaelis family, which is the author's natural milieu. The contrast is most skilfully suggested, and its influence, like that of a leitmotiv, knits together into a plausible whole the several dramas of the two children, strangers to one another, shut up together for a whole day; of Karen and Max Ebhardt; of Max and Mme Fisher; of Max and Naomi Fisher: until the carefully controlled surface of the book is felt to be underpinned by one of those cat's-cradles which, in life, cause us to exclaim: 'How small the world is!'

The plot itself has the fascinating ambiguity of the supernatural; caught up in something larger than themselves, outdistanced by their own acts, the characters rise to their creator's occasion in words that have the precise eloquence we have noticed in Miss Compton-Burnett. It was a master-stroke of imagination to have made the children, at the moments of crisis in the story, appear less innocent than most of the adults who surround them. (If we feel sometimes that these children use expressions which are beyond their years, it is because Miss Bowen's dialogue is, on the whole, far less stylised than that of Miss Compton-Burnett, who presents children in the same light.) And when words fail them at last, and they cling together with tears of disappointment and desolation, that is the author's moment of poetry—perhaps the best among the many she has imagined, both in this and other books.

Until *The Heat of the Day*, *The House in Paris* was Miss Bowen's largest, most far-reaching novel. It was eclipsed in public esteem by the later *Death of the Heart*, which is more direct, more scathing, and more consistently amusing. In a sense it is its author's most spirited book. Miss Bowen has always been able to make us laugh aloud by her portraits of second-rate people. Mark Linkwater (*To the North*), Mrs Vermont and Livvy (*The Last September*), are observed with the virulent exactitude of extreme distaste. The results are in the best tradition of feminine humour; but it is not till we come to the dreadful Heccomb family, in *The Death of the Heart*, that we find Miss Bowen really stamping on the accelerator. The section of this long novel entitled 'The Flesh' is indeed appallingly funny. The moral shoddiness, the callous opportunism, the tastelessness, the threadbare emotional background of this very ordinary English household of the provincial middle class, are rendered with a technical brilliance that astonishes. But it is, I think, possible to feel that the author has overweighted her book here: the last section is too short for what has gone before. My final impression of this novel is that it suffers from the author's having enjoyed herself too much in it: the control is less perfect than in *The House in Paris*, the invention spread thinner, the whole conception less poetically bold. And amusing as the Heccombs are, I prefer the passages of delicious observation, of humour less purely satiric, which abound elsewhere in these novels.

'What are men one is engaged to like?'
'Very worried and kind,' said Marda, blotting a sheet of her letter. 'Business-like, passionate, and accurate. When they press you against their chests a paper crackles, and when you sit up again to do your face and arrange your hair, they cough and pull out the paper, all folded and say: "While I think of it, I just wanted to consult you about this." Dinner services come crashing through the air like in a harlequinade. You feel you have been kissed in a shop. I cannot be adequate. I suggested writing to those public schools for vacancies for our three little boys, but that was not nice apparently. When you are engaged you live in the future, and a large part of the future is improper till it has happened.'

(*The Last September*)

Though seen through a woman's eyes, the men in these novels are more various than those of Miss Compton-Burnett. They tend, it is true, to be definitely either gentlemen or cads (Miss Bowen makes no bones about the reality of this distinction, which is part of her view of life); but there are intermediate types, such as Max Ebhart and Julian Tower, and on these she expends the best of her analytical subtlety. The following passage conveys, I think, her method of getting round a character:

> In fact, it was less the niece than the uncle that worried Julian: something in him that would not bring off the simplest relationship, that could be aware of any relationship only as something to be brought off; something hyperconscious of strain or falsity. This descent of an orphan child on his life might have been superficially comic, or even touching. But the disheartening density of Proust was superimposed for him on a clear page of Wodehouse. The poor child's approximation to what she took to be naturalness parodied his own part in an intimacy. She mortified him on his own account and on account of the woman so drearily nascent in her immaturity: he confronted again and again in her look, as she chattered and romped, the unavowable anxiety of the comedian. He was estranged from her, as though she were transparent, as he was estranged from almost all women, by a rather morbid consciousness of fraternity. After three days of her company, he felt like a pane of mean glass scrubbed horribly clean, like a pool dredged of its charming shadowy water-weeds. Those inexactitudes of desire that sent him towards Cecilia, those bright smoky movements of fancy became remote and impossible. Sobriety, peopled with nudes, became unseemly as a Turkish bath; he could look nowhere without confusion, least of all at himself.
>
> (*To the North*)

Miss Compton-Burnett would, almost certainly, have contrived this impression by a cross-fire of argument; but it should not be assumed (as it so often is) that dialogue is necessarily superior, as a method of exposition, to discursive analysis. Dialogue is of course always more dramatic than narrative, but as long as this is taken into account in planning the lay-out of the book, there is no moral obligation to put into dialogue what you prefer to explain in' your own' words.

*   *   *

[Several pages of detailed discussion on *The Heat of the Day*, which involve no comparisons with or comments on I. Compton-Burnett, are omitted here.–*Ed*.]

*   *   *

The fascination exercised by her novels is apt to make one forget that Miss Bowen is also a voluminous writer of short stories. Of these the longest are also distinctly the most successful. *The Disinherited*, for instance, belongs to the best of her work. But she is the kind of writer who needs space for her best effects, and although her shorter stories are executed with epigrammatic verve and adroitness, their qualities tend to be of the magazine order. If one regrets these *tours de force*, it is because, in a writer of Miss Bowen's attainments, one resents any lowering of standards; also—and more importantly—because the faint whiff of vulgarity which rises from the pages of a volume like *Look at all Those Roses* can also be discerned, as a disintegrating factor, in *The Death of the Heart*.

However, in her latest collection of stories, *The Demon Lover*, as well as in *The Heat of the Day*, this disheartening fault is altogether to seek. Indeed, I wonder if Miss Bowen has ever written better, or risen to greater heights of imaginative excellence, than in things like *The Happy Autumn Fields* (she manages the supernatural without a hint of whimsy), *The Inherited Clock*, *Ivy Gripped the Steps*, *Sunday Afternoon*. In the last-named story she joins hands with Miss Compton-Burnett, whose style may be said, without derogatory intent, to have influenced the whole tone of the dialogue. Yet 'influence' is probably the wrong term to use here: mature writers do not imitate those with whom they have not already more than a little in common, and it is fairer to regard Miss Bowen and Miss Compton-Burnett as complementary to one another in the positions from which each has chosen to evolve her complex, but neatly exhaustive, art.

*   *   *

Wider in scope but less perfect than Jane Austen, superior to Susan Ferrier (whom in many ways she strongly resembles), at her best the equal of Charlotte Brontë, Elizabeth Bowen is already assured of a distinguished place in any civilisation capable of appreciating, say, *Middlemarch*. The rich background of Anglo-Irish life from which she springs must be presumed in the main responsible for her extraordinary gifts: there is little object in probing further in this direction. A dedicated novelist, she adds, in each successive book, to the private history of English life in our times.

Miss Compton-Burnett's value is easier to assess, because she has set herself a more special, and perhaps on the whole a still harder task. Though her scene is apparently so confined, the moral implications of her art reach into every corner, not only of her own world, but of those worlds the existence of which she only implies. That is the advantage of the high degree of 'abstraction' involved by her method: it achieves universality by dint of excluding what is not essential to the completeness of the design. Like an expert piquet player, she prefers the bird in her hand to the dubious number she might pick up in the *talon*. The results are self-evident, timeless, therefore proof against the hysteria of fashion and the blight of political theory.

Inclinations, Secker & Warburg, 1949.

Mario Praz

THE NOVELS OF IVY COMPTON-BURNETT

ROBERT LIDDELL, IN his *A Treatise on the Novel* published in 1947, assigned a position of the first rank in modern fiction, and not only English fiction, to the novels of Ivy Compton-Burnett, and has taken up the subject again in a little volume, *The Novels of I. Compton-Burnett*, published by Gollancz in London; in order, he says, 'to save our literary generation from the discredit of not having issued one book solely devoted to the novels of this writer'.

Compton-Burnett began to publish in 1911 with *Dolores*, a juvenile work that the author would like forgotten and that surely would give a false idea of her art: it might be taken, says Liddell, for a rather stiff translation of a Russian novel or Greek tragedy; but already, in this incongruous comparison, is forecast one of the characteristics of the mature novelist.

After an interval of fifteen years, Compton-Burnett began an uninterrupted production that from 1925 to 1955 amounted to fourteen novels. It did not take that many for E. M. Forster to establish himself as a figure of the first rank in English letters: why then is it that Compton-Burnett, who in her own way is no less representative than Forster, has won only a slight fame in England, to say nothing of abroad, where she is nearly unknown?

In her own country she is spoken of only through hearsay, and the idea of her is quite inaccurate: sometimes she is classified as a humorous writer, sometimes as a diverting eccentric of the type of Ronald Firbank whose novels have very little to do with real life, sometimes as the idol of an esoteric cult, oracle of the coterie. To tell the truth Compton-Burnett has very much the appearance of pythoness or sybil: the picture of her which accompanies Liddell's monograph shows her as thin and wrinkled, with sharp features and fierce eyes under a helmet of gray hair rising on her temples in two Michelangelesque wings: the photograph was evidently inspired by certain portraits by Rembrandt. If physiognomies tell anything, from such a face we certainly could not

expect airy arabesques in the Firbank manner nor poetic atmos-
pheres *à la* Virginia Woolf: rather something tragic, severe, and
harsh. This is a Dantesque face, the visage of one who has beheld
an inferno. Not an inferno in the high style of Dante, but the
inferno that rages behind the respectable façades of many a
bourgeois house of the late Victorian period: this is precisely the
universal theme of the novels of Compton-Burnett, which the
seriousness of their author, her absence of indulgence in facile
effects, saves from falling into the melodramatic or the terato-
logical—that vast category to which a Catulle Mendès and a
Carolina Invernizio belong.

Neither to this nor indeed to any other category belongs this
novelist: it is difficult to say whom she resembles. Many times her
dialogues call to mind the stichomythia of Greek drama, and the
trivial details in which the tone of voice of the speakers is under-
lined, the way in which they themselves seem to present stage
directions for their dialogues, can recall Henry James; but these
are vague comparisons. In her limiting her observations to a
particular social setting, in her concentrating on the dialogues and
paying scant attention to setting, it can be said she has affinities
with the school of Jane Austen and Mrs Gaskell.

But in Compton-Burnett there is something profoundly sinister
that you would search for in vain in Austen or Gaskell, that you
might discover in James, and that you certainly feel in Greek
plays. In these plays we are so accustomed to parricides, incests,
monstrous loves, that we would be surprised to find a play in
which they were absent; but when in Dickens we find recogni-
tions of foundlings and other such events of classical drama we
immediately say that we are in the presence of melodrama, of the
unreal, of the material of serial romances.

Now in the novels of Compton-Burnett things happen much
more gross than in the novels of Dickens, yet we are not struck
by a sense of the improbable. Introduce into a Victorian drawing-
room the climate of the first stasimon of the *Choephori* of Aeschylus: 'The earth generates many fearful scourges. . . . But who
dares to speak of the audacity of men and women who smother
in their hearts those violent passions whose consequences for
mortals are deadly?' Although the result of this introduction could

be caricature, in Compton-Burnett it attains the grim efficacy of the collages of a Max Ernst: at the feet of a bourgeois bed breaks a stormy ocean and all around is the terrible odour of shipwreck.

The Victorian period was the classical age of the unhappy family: parental tyrannies, suppressed hatreds, sacrificed lives, unvoiced griefs, crimes concealed by respectability. Only recall the familiar history of certain celebrated English writers of the 1800's: the dramatic and tragic parish of Haworth in the moors of Yorkshire, where the Brontë sisters suffered and created; think of the other grim parish where Tennyson's father secretly drank and broke out in frightful rages; of the parish where Samuel Butler spent his youth, where evil had the face of cold cruelty and self-satisfied hypocrisy; think of the house in Wimpole Street where Elizabeth Barrett waited like Andromeda for someone to liberate her from the beloved monster who was her father; or think of the other grim scene at Denmark Hill where Effie Ruskin struggled between an impotent husband and a wicked mother-in-law.

Oh, indeed; there were fearful scourges in that self-satisfied Victorian society, as probably in every society, but there they were rendered more sinister by the patina of respectability which had to be safeguarded no matter what the cost. I do not know if any among my readers have ever seen the *Fall River Legend* as presented in other years by the New York City Ballet. It captured precisely the quintessence of that grim Victorianism which provides the material for the fifteen Compton-Burnett novels.

Whoever thought that sexual passion, so repressed in that period, is the dominant theme of those novels, would be deceiving himself; the dominant theme is the lust for power. In every family there are tyrants, victims, and witnesses; secret Calvaries, un-spoken hatreds, struggles to bend the will of another who, according to the ethos of the time, owed a tribute of submission, struggles to obtain favours in a will. All this happened between 1885 and 1901. Women wore bustles, and men, bowler hats and high collars; but it is as if they were acting out a much older drama, Greek or Elizabethan, in modern costume: the *Oresteia, Arden of Feversham, The Duchess of Malfi*, these are revived under gaslight, among the bastard furniture and decorative palms of a *fin-de-siècle* drawing room.

But Compton-Burnett does not give any indication of the settings, she is not a bourgeois of the stamp of Balzac minutely inventorying accessories: she thinks that people from force of habit are unaware of their surroundings, and does not distract the reader with them (as if a character at the moment of committing suicide realised he had before his eyes an enchanting view). Compton-Burnett is not a contemplative; she cares only about watching over the growth of those curious thick-leaved plants, the arid and spiny tribe of her creation—not that all of them are dry or thorn-protected in truth, for in her vast galleries the tender of heart, the simple, and the affectionate are not missing. Naturally; for to imagine that all the world is evil is an error as enormous as the opposite.

But the good are not necessarily rewarded; on the contrary, Compton-Burnett—not from reading de Sade, but from experience—seems to conclude that evil frequently remains unpunished. *Elders and Betters*, for example, ends with the triumph of the evildoers. The reviewer in the *New Statesman* (the novel appeared in 1944) would have preferred an ending more in conformity with traditional justice. The novelist objected: 'The reviewer in the *New Statesman* wanted the wickedness punished, but I hold that it is not punished, and this accounts for culpability. When there is the probability of being punished, most of us avoid wrongdoing.' A confession that seems cynical, as are many of the aphorisms scattered throughout the novels, in which Compton-Burnett amuses herself by turning upside down the popular wisdom of proverbs. And thus it amuses her to contravene the laws of verisimilitude. But, observes Liddell, does not life offer examples of cases even stranger than those in the novels of Compton-Burnett? Didn't we read even in the chronicles of England long ago of a brother and sister happily married? This is the status of Christian and Sophia Stace in one of these novels: a deliberate irony of the novelist that life itself confirms.

Yes, strange things happen; but Compton-Burnett, the most impersonal of narrators, does not comment; she is not even concerned to draw full-length portraits of her characters; she lets them speak, records their conversations with the impartiality of a tape-recorder; the comments of the chorus are provided by governesses, servants, relations. And the result is that the exploration made by Compton-Burnett with her lantern into the underground cellars and dungeons of the family is the most complete, as Liddell asserts, that exists in literature. 'Her distinction,' he says, 'is to be one of the definitive writers, one of those who tell us the extreme things of which the human spirit, in certain directions, is capable.' And also of those who have penetrated most truthfully into the minds of childhood. In *Men and Wives*, Liddell also says, 'the group of minor characters alone contains more memorable individuals than could be assembled from the complete works of any other living novelist.'

We note, incidentally, how often the characters of Compton-Burnett bear famous literary names. Chaucer, Bunyan, Francis Bacon, Herrick, Marlowe, Donne, Smollett, Swift, Lamb, Edgeworth, Shelley ... we do not find Shakespeare, but might not even this be a deliberate irony of the author, to give such illustrious names to persons who could be met every day? Summing up, one might say that Compton-Burnett follows that trend towards the democratisation of the heroic which is typical of Victorian fiction. Here are the themes of Greek tragedy—peripateia, anagnorisis, and catharsis (the novels often close on a tone of reconciliation and pardon) introduced into an apparently respectable bourgeois world; instead of wearing buskins, tragedy dons slippers; here are illustrious names given to everyday persons; here is a style that under a humble and even negligent surface hides an uncommon figurative efficiency; here is this sibyl, lips compressed like a suction plug, who looks like an English spinster you could encounter in a *pensione* in Assisi. We confess that she almost frightens us—frightens us more than that poor devil of a Marquis de Sade.

Here are the titles of her novels; one is as good as another and all are recommended: *Pastors and Masters*, 1925, *Brothers and Sisters*, 1929, *Men and Wives*, 1931, *More Women than Men*, 1933, *A House and Its Head*, 1935, *Daughters and Sons*, 1937, *A Family and a Fortune*, 1939, *Parents and Children*, 1941, *Elders and Betters*, 1944, *Manservant and Maidservant*, 1947, *Two Worlds and Their*

Ways, 1949, *Darkness and Day*, 1951, *The Present and the Past*, 1953, *Mother and Son*, 1955. One of the most acute English critics of today, V. S. Pritchett, has said that the characters of Compton-Burnett 'more than speak, they carve their epitaphs on their tombs. They speak like brilliant skeletons come out of their closets.' The suspicion can arise, in the last analysis, that certain verses of Eliot's *The Waste Land* could be adapted to the world of Compton-Burnett:

> And bones cast in a little low dry garret,
> Rattled by the rat's foot only, year to year.

In the annals of magic, a witch can turn into a mouse and a mouse into a witch. This, with all due respect for the stature of a little-known novelist—whom Liddell would call eminent.

RAI Radio (Televisione Italiana) April 1, 1955.*

* A shortened form of this lecture appeared in *Storia della letteratura inglese* (Florence: Sansoni, 1960).

Angus Wilson

THE NOVELS OF IVY COMPTON-BURNETT

MISS COMPTON-BURNETT'S isolation from contemporary novelists is surely a most exact measure of the failure of the modern English novel. This failure is now a very worn-out critical theme. It threatens to become the most tedious of King Charles's heads and it should undoubtedly be avoided by any critic who does not wish to become as boring as Mr Dick. It inevitably arises, however, in any estimation of Miss Compton-Burnett's work.

The debate on the English novel's decline now runs like clockwork. We are cut off from our traditional roots, says the critic, the soil from which our greatness sprang has been weakened by artificial experiments. Without experiment, comes the reply, there can be no new growth, the soil will be clogged and choked with weeds. Surely, says the inevitable third and sensible critic, we may make use of all that experiment has taught us, may indeed experiment ourselves, without losing contact with our good old English tradition, the true husbandry needs old and new alike. The simile, though undistinguished, is, I think, justly used, for the debate on the decline of the novel has the same familiarity, the same echo of stale wireless discussions as the debate on the use of artificial manures. Yet, if the sensible third voice is right and I think we must concede it to be so, Miss Compton-Burnett seems alone in following its call. Her novels are deeply entrenched in the great tradition of the English novel, or rather, in the great traditions, for this much vaunted single tradition is an invention of obtuse and undiscriminating traditionalists. Miss Compton-Burnett is also a great experimentalist: she has rigorously adapted form and language to accord with her aims, which is surely the only serious experiment to be considered. And yet she stands so alone in a wilderness of dreary imitated dead experiment and dismal imitated dead tradition. The unique vigour, the formidable strength of her books does not come only from her ethic, her healthy acceptance of life, but is a direct expression of her creative

E

vitality. Her living art which should be an oak in a contemporary forest, stands out in its isolation, almost theatrically monolithic, like Stonehenge on Salisbury Plain.

To praise so highly is not indeed to say that the greatness of her achievement can be easily estimated, nor even that it can be absolutely asserted. She inherits and uses so many of the themes and manners of the nineteenth-century golden age of the novel. She has explored and made her own the aesthetic ethic, the touchstone of goodness in taste, decorum and sincerity which was once for all stated by Jane Austen and then miraculously expanded by James and not inconsiderably ornamented by Virginia Woolf and Forster. She can make humours into personalities compelling our childish horror, demanding our sympathy by their own childish pathos. Here she moves easily in the world not only of Sir Walter Elliot and Lady Catherine de Burgh, but of Mr Pecksniff and Mr Dorrit, of the Duc de Guermantes and the Baron de Charlus. She explores the stuff of personality, its fictions and its onion peelings of reality; and like the great nineteenth-century novelists, she exploits hypocrisy and false sincerity in humanity in order to discuss truth. These connections with the great novelists have, I think, been remarked upon by other critics. What, so far as I know, has not been noted is her likeness to a more improbable nineteenth-century writer—Oscar Wilde. There is, nevertheless, something strangely akin in their combination of the language and wit of high comedy with the plots of melodrama. She does not, of course, lapse so easily into the language of melodrama as Wilde, but there are purple passages in her work which are by no means intended ironically. Finally, it seems to me, that in the total statement of her novels, in what is insufficiently but conveniently described as her 'acceptance', she develops straight from the great agnostic artists of the last century. I use the word 'artists' here to denote the spiritual battle fought out in a Christian society. It seems customary to call her ethic pagan, and Mr Liddell*, her latest critic and great admirer, tries to define her novels in the terms of Greek tragedy. The attempts seem to me too grandiose and too remote, by asserting the wrong 'too much' about her work he

---

* *The Novels of I. Compton-Burnett* by Robert Liddell. (Gollancz, £0.60p).

ends by making too little of it. To use the word 'pagan' about any modern person is at best a vague term of differentiation, allowable perhaps to Christians confused by varieties of unbelief; to use it as a term of praise is unhistorical and misleading. It does not help in understanding Housman or Hardy, it helps even less in understanding Miss Compton-Burnett. The Christian surrounding of her world is more decayed, more punfunctory than that of George Eliot, and her answer is at once less consciously and culturally agnostic then George Eliot's, and also less unconsciously Christian than the burden of Evangelical duty that George Eliot carried. Nevertheless the Christian ruins are the backcloth of her family dramas—Establishment, orders of society, feeble ends of Christian ethics. When she portrays belief she does so with the same understanding and dignified rejection as George Eliot. For all her craggy isolation, for all the icy winds that seem at times to howl through her dialogue, there is a warmth, a sense of comedy at its highest level remaining at the end of many of her novels that makes her acceptant view of life seem strangely like the human realism of Tolstoy's best novels.

I have purposely allowed myself to bandy great names so freely, for it is only so, I think, that we can begin to see the difficulties of estimating Miss Compton-Burnett's place as a novelist. Her intention is very high, her handling of the dialogue medium she has chosen is masterly, her range is only in a rather superficial sense narrow, yet there are few, I think, who could happily feel that her total work, or indeed any of her individual novels, is great in the sense that we apply this word to Jane Austen, Dickens, George Eliot, Tolstoy or Proust. In some degree this is simply the difficulty of applying to a contemporary author judgement which is made up of qualities observed in novelists of the past. This difficulty, however, should not be very serious with Miss Compton-Burnett, whose work as we have seen bears such a close relationship to those very novelists. In some degree we may be unwilling to apply the word 'great' to a novelist whose works are unlikely ever to be popular as were those of Dickens or George Eliot. That there is some element of this in our difficulty seems likely when we compare her to Henry James—the comparison seems at once more allowable than any of the others we have made. Nevertheless I doubt if we will feel satisfied to place them on the same level. Yet if we do admit this distrust of an author with a limited appeal to be more than a sentimentalism, we shall have to explain what element is lacking in an unpopular author that contributes to 'greatness'. We cannot make the naïve charge of limited range of observation or of social scene, for we should have to reject our corner-stone, Jane Austen. Some critics, I suppose, would claim that Miss Compton-Burnett has lived cut off from her time; not only in the narrow sense that she does not write of contemporary life or that her world is a dead social unit—the late Victorian family—but on a deeper spiritual level. She has not been touched, they would suggest, by the fresh vision of original sin that has come to us in the last forty years. It is surely exactly this modernity of vision, however, which separates her agnosticism from that of George Eliot, as it does Mr T. S. Eliot's Christianity from Victorian Christianity. Finally, there are those who would refuse her greatness simply because she was working in the medium of the novel. The novel is a dead art, they would assert, we cannot therefore expect any more great novelists. Most of such critics, however, would admit that the novel is only dead if we are speaking of its traditional form, its future lies in new developments which will free the imagination. It can hardly be on this ground then that Miss Compton-Burnett can be denied greatness, for no one has rejected the old forms or evolved a new one more satisfactorily.

The truth, I believe, does not lie in any of these usual generalisations about content or form. Miss Compton-Burnett is unique not only in her difference from contemporary novelists and her superiority to them, but unique among novelists generally. And it is the peculiar quality of her remarkable talent that she immediately invites comparison with the great and yet cannot attain that status. From *Pastors and Masters* onwards—I see no reason to discuss *Dolores* since she does not do so herself—she consciously asserts her concern with the highest themes of the novel and demonstrates her special approach to them. It is a consciousness of importance, a direct statement of intention that allows for a thousand nuances, a host of subtleties, but allows of no serious development. Development comes not from conscious overtones, but from unconscious themes and conflicts and symbols. With *Pastors and Masters*, with Henry Bentley and the Merrys, she emerged full grown before a world that had no practice in recognising such a phenomenon. That her reputation has grown as more and more discerning critics have discovered her adult powers is not surprising, nor that those who have recognised her should proselytize her work and judge their friends by their reception of it. An adult writer of high seriousness is not so common a phenomenon that we can make her less than a touchstone of taste. There have, of course, been changes in her work; she has developed her children, she has developed her servants, in her latest novel, *Mother and Son*, she develops a cat, she allows herself an occasional comment now amid the flow of brilliant dialogue and the odd truncated personal descriptions, her style, though still curiously jerky in places, moves more easily. But these are not developments of the inner core of her writing; she need never have introduced what Mr Liddell calls her choruses of children and servants, she need never have smoothed out the awkwardnesses of her sentences, and she could still have ranked with the greatest. As it is, from the very first, we have had enough and more than enough to satisfy us, novels being as they are today. Nevertheless we have not had that inner development, that gradual unconscious change that we find between *Nicholas Nickleby* and *Our Mutual Friend*, or between *Scenes of Clerical Life* and *Middlemarch*, which we rightly associate with great novelists. Like other changes, these are not necessarily to be called progress; *The Ambassadors* is not necessarily better than *Portrait of a Lady* nor *Mansfield Park* than *Pride and Prejudice*. If it is for progress that we ask, it may well be said that *More Women than Men* is better than *Pastors and Masters*, and *A Family and a Fortune* or *A House and Its Head* better still. Indeed, in point of omission of distracting elements and of formal arrangement, her latest novel *Mother and Son* excels all the others. Fundamentally, however, her novels remain the same: she presents us with a whole view of life and conveys that whole view in a subtle and convincing way, but she does not tell us more of it or show it to us from another side, or make us feel or think about it more deeply than she did from the very start. It is thus, I think, that her work misses greatness, but misses it probably so narrowly that we are constantly urged to set her novels beside the master-pieces of the past.

This sameness of statement, complete yet never new, is surely the reason why many critics of discernment fail to appreciate her work. There are many readers, of course, who lack either wit or intellectual discipline to make contact with her novels. There are, however, people of wit and intelligence who find the dish monotonous, or others again like Miss Hansford Johnson who appreciate her work but can yet, as Mr Liddell is at pains to point out, lose their way in the labyrinth of her plots. This, I believe, is because of this underlying sameness, for there is certainly no other monotony. Each book contains characters so different, so completely lifelike that any attempt, like Mr Liddell's, to categorise them into tyrants or victims tells us nothing of any importance about them. Matty Seaton, cruel, brutal, that occasional real life person who is larger than life, clever and understanding, refuses to be categorised as a tyrant, and she certainly has nothing to do with the other tyrants, Harriet Haslam or Sophia Stace or Miranda Hume or Duncan Edgeworth or Sir Jesse Sullivan. It is useless for the critic to try his usual trick of categorising the events or the characters, for life is not susceptible to moral category, has no finality of event except death and that, as Miss Compton-Burnett never ceases to tell us, is only final to those who die and even then in quite different ways. There are, of course, goats and sheep, and in accordance with the great tradition of Miss Austen they are betrayed by nuances alone, but these nuances are not such constant tests in Miss Compton-Burnett's world as in Jane Austen's, not even so constant as they are in Forster's or Virginia Woolf's. There are the great 'humorous' figures like Sophia or Josephine or Matty or Rosebery Hume, figures with the outlines of Dickens's world, but though we know them to be somewhere on the wrong side of the fence, we must never build our fences too exactly. In Rosebery, the son of her new novel, *Mother and Son*, a certain sort of moralising, humourless, playful, heightened speech speaks against him or at the most calls for our pity, yet in Justine Gaveston we can see that the same tone speaks for 'goodness', and in Luce Sullivan for something in between. It is this ambiguity of personal values, I think, that makes the nature of her plots so essential to her novels. Much objection has been made to what is called their 'melodrama'—incest, illegitimacy, occasional murder. They are, of course, familiar mechanisms of novel narrative and if Miss Compton-Burnett used them purely formally as mechanical devices I do not think it would be objectionable. She has, however, in her radio discussion with Miss Jourdain, stated that she believes them to be real ingredients of a great deal of family life—sometimes as skeletons revealed, sometimes as skeletons for ever hidden. This view I entirely accept. It has been my experience that most middle-class families have some 'secret' of this kind in their midst. On grounds of realism also, then, they do not seem to me objectionable. If, however, we examine the nature of this 'melodrama' more closely we will find surely that it is an integral element in the whole ambiguity which is at the centre of her view of human values. The revelation of incest and of illegitimacy must mean that the members of a family have to see themselves anew as different people in exactly the most important sense that exists in the family unit—they are no longer sons and daughters, or they are not only sons and daughters of their parents but brothers and sisters as well. And if, as so often happens, they later find that the revelation was untrue, they must once again revert to their former view of their personalities, but the former view can never be what it was before because they have learned in between to see the whole of their world from a different angle. It is, of course, the common theme of Shakespearean comedy. Its final effect is to question at its roots the whole conception of 'personality', to consider it only as relative. And this, of course, is the essential of Miss Compton-Burnett's attitude. What, in fact, are we to make of personality or event at all, when illegitimacy so often proves us to be other than we thought, or when false report has made us digest a cataclysm that never occurred? Perhaps, we are led to conclude that relationship, the fundamental family relationship which rules her books, does not matter at all, when Christian and Sophia are sister and brother as well as husband and wife, or seem to be; or when Edmund Lovat seems to have married his daughter and has not; but who could say that it did not matter to Rosebery that Miranda was his mother even if Julius was not his father. Sometimes relationship is vital and sometimes it is not, is the answer. And so it is with everything else, with death, with malice, with arrogance, with charity, with patronage, with plain speaking, with lying, they may be good or they may not, they may be final or they may be transient. Nothing can be judged except in its context, and then only with reservation. In *Mother and Son*, for example, Miranda praises her son in these words, 'He would not do little wrong things behind my back; he would not do them any more than the great ones; and that is a rare thing.' Yet in the same book, Hester Wolsey does great wrong and her friend Emma Greatheart says, 'I will think the one thing, that she has known the depths, and that I have seen her knowing them. It is a good thing experience is ennobling. I believe she is becoming a little ennobled.' If we cannot judge of the good and the bad, we cannot also judge of the important and the unimportant. We can know, perhaps, that Dulcia Bode and Faith Crammer are as unimportant as they are comic, but this is exceptional levity on the author's part. Who can say whether Rosebery who looms so large is more important, even as a literary character, than his supposed father Julius, or Matty Seaton than her sister Blanche? We might as well try to judge between Vronsky and Anna, Karenin or Levin. The manner in which Miss Compton-Burnett so wonderfully suggests real life is, in fact, so similar to that of Tolstoy—Levin's sudden perception of religious truth which seems momentarily so decisive and yet is the next moment gone, the falsity of the apparently basic moments in Anna's life with Vronsky—change and false change, climaxes that are transient, chance remarks that are final, trivialities that take up more attention and energy than death or disaster. It is not that Miss Compton-Burnett is less plumb at the centre of life than her great predecessor, but only that Tolstoy gives us aspects of this centre from a hundred different, revolving mirrors that almost bewilder us by their changing reflections, while she has only one mirror, clear and full, but unchanging. It is, nevertheless, a mirror to be deeply grateful for.

London Magazine, July, 1955.

Nathalie Sarraute

CONVERSATION AND SUB-CONVERSATION

WHO TODAY WOULD dream of taking seriously, or even reading the articles that Virginia Woolf wrote shortly after the First World War on the art of the novel? Their naïve confidence, their innocence of another age, would only elicit a smile. 'It is difficult,' she wrote with enviable candour, 'not to take it for granted that the modern practice of the art is somehow an improvement upon the old.'. . . . The tools used by classical writers were 'simple', their materials were 'primitive', and their masterpieces, in her opinion, had 'an air of simplicity'. 'But compare their opportunities with ours!' she said. And added proudly that, 'for the moderns,' the point of interest would 'very likely lie in the dark places of psychology'.

No doubt she had much to excuse her: *Ulysses* had just appeared. *In a Budding Grove* was about to receive the Goncourt Prize. She herself was working on *Mrs Dalloway*. Quite obviously, she lacked perspective.

But for most people, the works of Joyce and Proust already rise up in the distance like witnesses of a past epoch, and the day will soon come when no one will visit these historical monuments otherwise than with a guide, along with groups of school children, in respectful silence and somewhat dreary admiration. For several years now interest in 'the dark places of psychology' has waned. This twilight zone in which, hardly thirty years ago, we thought we saw the gleam of real treasures, has yielded us very little, and we are obliged to acknowledge that, when all is said and done, this exploration, however bold and well carried out it may have been, however extensive and with whatever elaborate means, has ended in disappointment. The most impatient and most daring among the novelists were not long in declaring that the game was not worth the candle and that they preferred to turn their efforts in another direction. The word 'psychology' is one that no present-day writer can hear spoken with regard to himself without casting his eyes to the ground and blushing. It has something slightly ridiculous, antiquated, cerebral, limited, not to say, pretentiously silly about it. Intelligent people, all progressive minds, to whom an imprudent writer would dare admit his secret hankering for the 'dark places of psychology'—but who would dare to do so?— would undoubtedly reply with pitying surprise: 'Indeed! so you still believe in all that? . . .' Since the appearance of the 'American novel' and the profound, blinding truths with which the literature of the absurd has continued to swamp us, there are not many left who believe in it. All Joyce obtained from those dark depths was an uninterrupted flow of words. As for Proust, however doggedly he may have separated into minute fragments the intangible matter that he brought up from the subsoil of his characters, in the hope of extracting from it some indefinable, anonymous substance which would enter into the composition of all humanity, the reader has hardly closed the book before, through an irresistible movement of attraction, all these particles begin to cling to one another and amalgamate into a coherent whole with clear outlines, in which the practised eye of the reader immediately recognises a rich man of the world in love with a kept woman, a prominent, awkward, gullible doctor, a parvenue bourgeoise or a snobbish 'great lady,' all of whom will soon take their places in the vast collection of fictitious characters that people his imaginary museum.

What enormous pains to achieve results that, without contortions and without hairsplitting, are obtained, shall we say, by Hemingway. And this being the case, if he handles them with equal felicity, why object to the fact that he uses the same tools that served Tolstoy in such good stead?

But there's no question of Tolstoy! Today, eighteenth- and even seventeenth-century writers are constantly being held up to us as models. And should some die-hard, at the risk of his life, continue to want to explore gropingly the 'darker sides,' he is immediately referred back to *The Princess of Cleve* and *Adolph*. He should read the classics a bit! Would he for a moment claim to penetrate farther than they did into the depths of the soul, or with such ease and grace, with so keen, so light a touch?

Indeed, as soon as a writer renounces the legacy of those whom, thirty years ago, Virginia Woolf called 'moderns' and, disdaining the liberties (the 'facilities', he would say) that they conquered, succeeds in capturing a few soul reactions couched in the pure, simple, elegant lines that characterise the classical style, he is praised to the skies. With what alacrity, what generosity, people exert themselves to discover an abundance of inexpressible sentiments beneath his reticence and silence, to see reserve and contained strength in the prudence and abstinence that are forced upon him by constant concern for maintaining the 'figure' of his style.

However, the unfortunate die-hard who, being unconcerned by the indifference and reproval awaiting him, persists nevertheless in digging in these dark regions, in the hope of extracting from them a few particles of some unknown substance, does not, for all that, enjoy the peace of mind that his independence and disinterestedness should ensure him.

Frequently doubts and scruples slacken his endeavours. For where is he to find and be able to examine these secret recesses that attract him, if not in himself, or in the persons in his immediate circle whom he feels he knows well and whom he imagines he resembles? And the tiny, evanescent movements they conceal blossom out preferably in immobility and withdrawal. The din of actions accomplished in broad daylight either drowns or checks them.

But he is well aware, as he observes himself and his fellow-creatures from his inner sanctum, steeping in the protective liquor of his tightly-sealed little jar, that, on the outside, very important things (perhaps—and he tells himself this with anguish —the only really important things) are happening: men who are probably very different from him, as well as from his family and friends, men who have other fish to fry than to hover solicitously over their innermost quakings, and in whom, moreover, it would seem that deep suffering, deep, simple joys, powerful, very evident needs, must quell these very subtle tremors, men towards whom he feels drawn, whom, often, he admires, are acting and struggling; and he knows that, to be at peace with his conscience and meet the requirements of his time, it is with them and not with himself or those like him that he should be concerned.

But if, having torn himself away from his jar, he should

attempt to turn his attention towards these men and make them
come to life in his books, he is assailed by fresh misgivings. His
eyes, having become accustomed to semi-darkness, are dazzled
by the garish light of the outside. As a result of examining only
the tiny space about him, of staring lengthily at one spot, they
have become magnifying lenses that are incapable of taking in
vast expanses at one time. Long maceration in his jar has made him
lose his innocent freshness. He has seen how difficult it was, when
he examined closely some tiny recess in himself, to make an
inventory of all the things to be found there: not of any great
importance, he is well aware, more than often disappointing, but
concerning which a rapid examination, made from a distance,
would never have permitted him even to suspect their existence.
He consequently has the impression of not seeing these men from
the outside clearly. Their actions, which he respects and admires,
seem to him to be like wide-meshed netting: they let slip through
their large holes all this turbid, teeming matter to which he has
grown accustomed, and he is unable to break himself of the habit
of looking for the living substance, the, for him, only living substance; also, he is obliged to admit that he sees nothing in what
they bring back but large empty carcasses. These men whom he
would so like to know and make known, when he tries to show
them moving about in the blinding light of day, seem to him to
be nothing but well-made dolls, intended for the amusement of
children.

Furthermore, if it is a matter of showing characters from the
outside, devoid of all swarmings and secret tremors, and of
recounting their actions and the events that compose their story,
of telling stories about them, as he is so often incited to do (isn't
this, people continually tell him, the gift that best characterises
the real writer?), the cinema director, who disposes of means of
expression that are far better suited to this purpose and much
more powerful than his own, succeeds in easily surpassing him,
with less fatigue and loss of time for the spectator. And when it
comes to describing men's sufferings and struggles plausibly, to
making known all the frequently monstrous, almost unbelievable
iniquities that are committed, the journalist possesses the immense
advantage over him of being able to give to the fact he reports—

however unlikely they may seem—that look of authenticity which, alone, is capable of compelling the reader's credence.

Lacking encouragement, lacking confidence, with a frequently painful sense of guilt and boredom, he has no alternative, therefore, but to return to himself. But here, although he has plunged once more into his jar after this evasion, which is more than often imaginary—he is usually far too distrustful and discouraged in advance to venture outside—it would be painting far too black a picture of his situation, if we did not say that to his own astonishment and pretty rarely at that, he occasionally experiences moments of satisfaction and hope.

One fine day he hears that even out yonder, on the outside, not in those gloomy, solitary regions in which he is groping about, and into which the little company of moderns had once ventured, but in the rich, eternally fertile, well-populated and carefully cultivated lands where tradition continues to blossom in the sun, people have finally noticed that, after all, something is happening. Novelists whom nobody would ever accuse of making revolutionary claims are forced to recognise certain changes. One of the best contemporary English novelists, Henry Green, has pointed out that the centre of gravity of the novel has moved, that more and more importance is being given to dialogue. 'Today,' he writes, 'it is the best way to give the reader real life.' And he even predicts that it will be 'the principal support of the novel for a long time to come'.

In the silence that surrounds him, this simple statement is an olive branch for our die-hard. It makes him take heart immediately. It even revives his wildest dreams. No doubt, the explanation Mr Green gives of this change risks destroying all the promise contained in his remark: it is probably, he adds, because 'nowadays people have stopped writing letters. Instead, they use the telephone.' It is not to be wondered at then that, in their turn, characters in fiction should have become so talkative.

But this explanation is disappointing in appearance only. It should not be forgotten that Mr Green is English and it is well known that reserve often incites his countrymen to adopt a tone of playful simplicity when speaking of serious matters. Or perhaps it is a dash of humour. Perhaps, too, after making this bold statement, Henry Green experienced a certain fear: if he were to carry his investigation too far, where would it not lead him? Might he not eventually come to ask himself if this single indication of his were not a sign of profound disturbances that could lead to re-examination of the entire traditional structure of the novel? Might he not end by claiming that contemporary novel forms are cracking on all sides, and thus instigate, even invite, new techniques adapted to new forms? But the words 'new forms' and 'techniques' are even more immodest and embarrassing to pronounce than the word 'psychology' itself. They result immediately in your being accused of presumption and bumptiousness, and arouse, in both critics and readers, a feeling of mistrust and annoyance. It is consequently more proper and more prudent to limit oneself to mention of the telephone.

But however great our novelist's fears of appearing to yield to an enthusiasm that is suspect, he cannot be content with this explanation. For it is above all when he must make his characters speak that it seems to him that something is changing, and that it appears most difficult to avail himself of the methods that have been in current usage thus far. Between Henry Green's observation and his own impressions and reluctance there must be something more than mere coincidence. And from then on, everything changes: the confusion he senses is apparently not, as people tell him, and as he himself in his moments of depression is liable to think, that of senility, but of growth; his endeavours would seem to make him go forward in the direction of a vast general movement. And all the arguments used against those whom Virginia Woolf called moderns could be turned to their advantage.

But, people say, it is not possible to repeat what they did. Their techniques, in the hands of those who attempt to use them today, immediately become a device, whereas the traditional novel retains eternal youth. Without having to undergo any appreciable changes, its generous, supple forms continue to adapt themselves to all the new stories, all the new characters and new conflicts that appear in the societies that succeed one another, and it is in the novelty of these characters and conflicts that the principal interest and only valid renewal of the novel lie.

And it is true that we cannot repeat what Joyce or Proust did, even though Stendhal and Tolstoy are repeated every day to everybody's satisfaction. But isn't this, first of all, because the moderns displaced the essential interest of the novel? For them it ceased to lie in the enumeration of situations and characters or in the portrayal of manners and customs, but in the revelation of a new psychological subject-matter. Indeed, it is the discovery if only of a few particles of this subject-matter, which is an anonymous one, to be found in all men and in all societies, that constituted for them and continues to constitute for their successors, genuine renewal. To re-work after them this same material and, consequently, to use their methods without changing them in any way, would be quite as absurd as for supporters of the traditional novel to re-write with the same characters, the same plot and the same style, *The Red and the Black* or *War and Peace*.

On the other hand, the techniques used today with occasionally still excellent results by advocates of tradition, techniques invented by novelists of another day to explore the unknown material that fell within their range of vision, and which were perfectly adapted to this purpose, these techniques have ended by constituting a very strong, coherent system of conventions, which is well constructed and entirely closed; a universe that has its own laws and is self-sufficient. Through force of habit, by virtue of the authority conferred upon it, and because of the great works it has engendered, it has become a second nature. It has assumed a necessary, an eternal aspect. So much so that today still, those persons, whether writers or readers, who have been the most disturbed by all the upheavals that have been taking place for some time now outside its thick walls, as soon as they enter within them, docilely allow themselves to be confined there; they very soon feel quite at home, accept all limitations, conform to all restraints, and abandon all dreams of escape.

But by freeing themselves of its fetters, the moderns, who sought to tear themselves as well as their readers away from this system, lost the protection and security it offered. And the reader, being deprived of all his accustomed stakes and landmarks, removed from all authority, suddenly faced with an unknown substance, bewildered and distrustful, instead of blindly letting

himself go, as he so loves to do, was constantly obliged to con-
front what was shown him with what he could see for himself.

Just in passing, he must have been extremely surprised by the
opacity of the fictional conventions that had succeeded in con-
cealing for so long what should have been obvious to all eyes.
But once he had taken a good look and arrived at an independent
judgement, he was unable to stop there. At the same time that
they had awakened his powers of penetration, the moderns had
awakened his critical faculties and whetted his curiosity.

He wanted to look even further or, if preferred, even closer.
And he was not long in perceiving what was hidden beneath the
interior monologue: an immense profusion of sensations, images,
sentiments, memories, impulses, little larval actions that no inner
language can convey, that jostle one another on the threshold of
consciousness, gather together in compact groups, loom up all of
a sudden, then immediately fall apart, combine otherwise and
reappear in new forms, while unwinding inside us, like the
ribbon that comes clattering from a telescriptor slot, in an uninterrupted flow of words.

With regard to Proust, it is true that these groups composed
of sensations, images, sentiments and memories which, when
traversing or skirting the thin curtain of the interior monologue,
suddenly become visible from the outside, in an apparently
insignificant word, a mere intonation or a glance, are precisely
what he took such pains to study. But—however paradoxical
this may seem to those who, today, still reproach him for his
extreme minutiae—to us it appears already as though he had
observed them from a great distance, after they had run their
course, in repose and, as it were, congealed in memory. He tried
to describe their respective positions as though they were stars
in a motionless sky. He considered them as a sequence of causes
and effects which he sought to explain. He rarely—not to say,
never—tried to re-live them and make them re-live for the reader
in the present, while they were forming and developing, like so
many tiny dramas, each one of which has it adventures, its
mystery and its unforeseeable ending.

It was doubtless this that prompted Gide to say that he had
collected the raw material for a great work rather than achieved

the work itself, and brought upon him the serious reproach still made today by his opponents, of having gone in for 'analysis', that is to say, in the most original parts of his work, of having incited the reader to use his own intelligence, instead of giving him the sensation of re-living an experience, of accomplishing himself certain actions, without knowing too well what he is doing or where he is going—which always was and still is in the very nature of any work of fiction.

But isn't this like reproaching Christopher Columbus with not having constructed the port of New York?

Those who have followed him and who have wanted to try and make these subterranean actions re-live for the reader as they unfold, have met with certain difficulties. Because these inner dramas composed of attacks, triumphs, recoils, defeats, caresses, bites, rapes, murders, generous abandons or humble submissions, all have one thing in common: they cannot do without a partner.

Often it is an imaginary partner who emerges from our past experiences or from our day-dreams, and the scenes of love or combat between us, by virtue of their wealth of adventure, the freedom with which they unfold and what they reveal concerning our least apparent inner structure, can constitute very valuable fictional material.

It remains nonetheless true that the essential feature of these dramas is constituted by an actual partner.

For this flesh and blood partner is constantly nurturing and renewing our stock of experiences. He is pre-eminently the catalyser, the stimulant, thanks to whom these movements are set in motion, the obstacle that gives them cohesion, that keeps them from growing soft from ease and gratuitousness, or from going round and round in circles in the monotonous indigence of ruminating on one thing. He is the threat, the real danger as well as the prey that brings out their alertness and their suppleness; the mysterious element whose unforeseeable reactions, by making them continually start up again and evolve towards an unknown goal, accentuate their dramatic nature.

But at the same time that, in order to attain to this partner, they rise up from our darkest recesses towards the light of day, a certain fear forces them back towards the shadow. They make us think of the little grey roaches that hide in moist holes. They are ashamed and prudent. The slightest look makes them flee. To blossom out they must have anonymity and impunity.

They consequently hardly show themselves in the form of actions. For actions do indeed develop in the open, in the garish light of day, and the tiniest of them, compared with these delicate, minute inner movements, appear to be gross and violent: they immediately attract attention. All their forms have long since been examined and classified; they are subject to strict rules, to very frequent inspection. Finally, very obvious, well-known, frank motives, thick, perfectly visible wires make all this enormous, heavy machinery work.*

But lacking actions, we can use words. And words possess the qualities needed to seize upon, protect and bring out into the open these subterranean movements that are at once impatient and afraid.

They have in their favour their suppleness, their freedom, the iridescent richness of their shading, their transparency or their opaqueness.

* These gross motives, these vast, apparent movements, are usually all that is seen by both writers and readers, who are borne along by the movement of the action and spurred on by the plot in Behaviourist novels. They have neither time nor means—not having at their disposal a sufficiently delicate instrument of investigation—to see clearly the more fleeting, subtler movements that these grosser movements may conceal.

Indeed, we can understand the aversion these writers feel for what they call 'analysis', which, for them, would consist in pointing out these perfectly visible, frank motives, thus doing the reader's work for him and giving themselves the disagreeable impression of forcing already open doors.

It is nevertheless curious to observe that, to escape the boredom of going round and round in the narrow circle of customary actions, in which they find really nothing much left to be gleaned, seized with the desire natural to all writers to take their readers into unknown regions, and haunted, in spite of everything, by the existence of the 'dark places', but still firmly convinced that action by itself can reveal them, they make their characters commit unwonted, monstrous acts which the reader, comfortably settled in his own clear conscience, and finding nothing in these criminal acts that corresponds to what he has learned to see in his own conduct, regards with proud, horrified curiosity, then quietly thrusts aside to return to his own affairs, as he does every morning and every evening after reading his newspaper, without the heavy shadow that submerges his own dark places having lifted for a single second.

Their rapid, abundant flow, with its restless shimmer, allows the more imprudent of them to slip by, to let themselves be borne along and disappear at the slightest sign of danger. But they risk little danger. Their reputation for gratuitousness, lightness, inconsistency—they are, after all, pre-eminently the instruments of frivolous pastimes and games—protects them from suspicion and from minute examination: we are generally content to make purely formal verification of them; they are subject to rather lax regulations; they rarely result in serious sanctions.

Consequently, provided they present a more or less harmless, commonplace appearance, they can be and, in fact, without anyone taking exception, without the victim even daring to admit it frankly to himself, they often are the daily, insidious and very effective weapon responsible for countless minor crimes.

For there is nothing to equal the rapidity with which they attain to the other person at the moment when he is least on his guard, often giving him merely a sensation of disagreeable tickling or slight burning; or the precision with which they enter straight into him at his most secret and most vulnerable points and lodge in his innermost recesses, without his having the desire, the means, or the time, to retort. But once they are deposited inside him, they begin to swell, to explode, they give rise around them to waves and eddies which, in turn, come up to the surface and spread out in words. By virtue of this game of actions and reactions that they make possible, they constitute a most valuable tool for the novelist.

And this, no doubt, is why, as Henry Green has noted, characters in fiction have become so talkative.

But this dialogue, which tends more and more, in the modern novel, to take the place left by action, does not adapt itself easily to the forms imposed by the traditional novel. For it is above all the outward continuation of subterranean movements which the author—and with him the reader—must make at the same time as the character, from the moment they form until the moment when, having been forced to the surface by their increasing intensity, to reach the other person and protect themselves from exterior dangers, they cloak themselves in the protective capsules of words.

Nothing, therefore, should break the continuity of these movements, and the transformation they undergo should be analogous to that sustained by a ray of light when it is refracted and curves as it passes from one sphere into another.

This being the case, there is really no justification for the heavy indentations and dashes with which we are accustomed to make a clear-cut separation between dialogue and what precedes it. Even the colon and quotation marks are still too apparent, and it is understandable that certain novelists (for instance, Joyce Cary) should strive to blend dialogue with its context—to the extent that this is possible—by simply marking the separation with a comma followed by a capital.

But even more awkward and hard to defend than indentations, dashes, colons and quotation marks, are the monotonous, clumsy, 'said Jeanne', 'answered Paul', with which dialogue is usually strewn; for contemporary novelists these are becoming more and more what the laws of perspective had become for painters just before Cubism: no longer a necessity, but a cumbersome convention.

Indeed, it is curious to see that, today, those very novelists who refuse to let themselves become what they consider to be needlessly disturbed; and who continue to use the devices of the old-fashioned novel with blithe assurance, seem unable to escape a certain feeling of uneasiness as regards this particular point. It is as though they had lost that certainty of being within their rights, that innocent unawareness that gives to the 'said, resumed, replied, retorted, exclaimed etc. . . .' with which Madame de Lafayette or Balzac so brightly studded their dialogues, that look of being securely where they belong, indispensable and perfectly as a matter of course, that makes us accept them without raising an eyebrow, without even noticing it, when we re-read these authors today. And compared to them, how self-conscious, anxious and unsure of themselves contemporary novelists seem, when they use these same formulas.

At times—like people who prefer to flaunt and even accentuate their faults to ward off danger and disarm their critics—they ostentatiously renounce the subterfuges used ingenuously by writers of the old school (which today seem to them to be too gross and too easy, and which consisted in constantly varying their formulas), and expose the monotony and clumsiness of this device by repeating tirelessly, with affected negligence or *naïveté*, 'said Jeanne', 'said Paul', 'said Jacques'; the only result being to fatigue and irritate the reader all the more.

At others, they tried to make these unfortunate 'said Jeanne', 'replied Paul', disappear, by following them, on every occasion, with repetitions of the last words of the dialogue: 'No, said Jeanne, no' or: 'It's finished, said Paul, it's finished.' This gives to the words the characters speak a solemn, emotional tone which obviously does not correspond to the author's intention. Then, again, they do away as much as possible with this cumbersome appendix by continually introducing the dialogue in a still more artificial way which we feel does not answer to any inner necessity: Jeanne smiled: 'I leave the choice to you', or: Madeleine looked at him: 'I was the one who did it.'

All these resorts to too apparent subterfuges, all these embarrassed attitudes, are a source of great cheer to followers of the moderns. They see in them premonitory signs, proof that something is falling apart, that there is filtering insidiously into the minds of the supporters of the traditional novel a doubt as to the merits of their rights, a scruple at entering into possession of their inheritance, which, without their realising it, make of them, as it were, the privileged classes before revolutions, the agents of future upheavals.

Indeed, it is not by mere chance that it should be at the moment when they use these short, apparently harmless formulas that they feel most ill at ease. For, in a way, these are symbols of the old regime, the point at which the old and the new conceptions of the novel separate most distinctly. They mark the site on which the novelist has always located his characters, that is, at a point as remote from himself as from the reader; there, where the players in a tennis match are to be found, while the novelist occupies the place of the umpire perched on his stool, supervising the game and announcing the score to the fans (in this case, the readers) seated on the side-lines.

Neither the novelist nor the readers leave their seats to play the game themselves, as though they were players.

And this remains true when the character expresses himself in the first person, as soon as he begins to follow his own statements with, 'I said,' 'I cried,' 'I replied,' etc. . . . . He shows by this that he himself does not perform, nor does he make his readers perform, the inner movements that prepare the dialogue, from the moment they originate until the moment when they appear externally, but that, keeping himself at a distance, he makes this dialogue start up in the presence of an insufficiently prepared reader whom he is obliged to warn.

Being thus on the outside and at a distance from his characters, the novelist can adopt devices that vary from those of the Behaviourists to those of Marcel Proust.

Like the Behaviourists, he can make his characters speak without any preparation while he remains at a distance, limiting himself to apparently recording their dialogues and thus giving the impression of allowing them to live lives of their own.

But nothing is more deceptive than this impression.

Because although the little appendix that the novelist makes follow their spoken words shows that the author gives his creatures their head, it recalls at the same time that he is keeping a firm hold on the reins. These: 'said', 'continued', etc. . . . . that are delicately inserted in the midst of the dialogue, or prolong it harmoniously, are quiet reminders that the author is still present, and that this fictional dialogue, despite its apparent independence, cannot do without him and stand alone in the air, the way theatrical dialogue does; they are the light but strong ties that bind and subject the style and tone of the characters to the style and tone of the author.

As for the famous *intaglio* implications that the supporters of this system think they obtain by giving no explanations, it would be interesting to ask the most experienced and most sensitive among their readers to tell sincerely what they perceive, when left to themselves, beneath the words spoken by the characters. How much do they guess of all those tiny actions that subtend and set the dialogue in motion, giving it its real meaning? Undoubtedly the suppleness, subtlety, variety and abundance of words permit the reader to sense movements underneath them that are more numerous, sharper and more secret than those he can discover underneath actions. We should nevertheless be surprised by the simplicity, the grossness and the approximation of his perceptions.

But it would be a mistake to blame the reader.

Because, to make this dialogue 'life-like' and plausible, these novelists give it the conventional form that it has in every-day life: it consequently reminds the reader too much of the dialogues he himself is accustomed to record hastily, without asking too many questions, without looking for hidden difficulties (he has neither the time nor the means to do so, and this is exactly what the author's work consists of) being content to perceive beneath the spoken words only what allows him to order his own conduct somehow or other, without lingering morbidly over vague, dubious impressions.

But better still, what the reader discovers beneath these fictional dialogues—however loaded with secret meanings their author may have wanted them to be—is not much compared with what he himself can discover when, as a participant in the game, with all his instincts of defence and attack aroused, excited and on the alert, he observes and listens to those with whom he is talking.

Above all, it is not much compared to what the spectator learns from theatrical dialogue.

Because theatrical dialogue, which needs no props, and during which the author does not constantly make us feel that he is present, ready to lend a hand; this dialogue, which must be self-sufficient and on which everything rests, is denser, tauter, more compact and at a higher tension than fictional dialogue: it also makes greater demands on the combined powers of the spectator.

But above all, the actors are there to do most of the work for him. Their entire task consists in recapturing and reproducing within themselves, at the cost of great, prolonged effort, the tiny, complicated inner movements that have propelled the dialogue that give it weight, distend and tauten it; and, by their gestures, their acting, their intonations, their silences, in communicating these movements to the audience.

Behaviourist novelists, who make abundant use of dialogue, set between brief indications or discreet commentaries, extend the novel dangerously near the domain of the theatre, where it is bound to be in a position of inferiority. And renouncing the means that the novel alone has at its disposal, they also renounce what makes it a unique art, or rather, simply an art.

There remains, then, the opposite method, Proust's, or recourse to analysis. This latter one, in any case, has the advantage over the former of maintaining the novel on its own ground, and using means that only the novel affords. It also tends to furnish the reader with what he has a right to expect from a novelist; that is, experience increased not in breadth (this may be had at less cost and more effectively through documents and news reports) but in depth. And above all, it is not conducive, under the cloak of so-called renovations, to an attachment to the past, but looks frankly towards the future.

As regards dialogue in particular, Proust himself, concerning whom it is not exaggeration to say that, more than any other novelist, he excelled in the very minute, exact, subtle, highly evocative descriptions of the play of features, the glances, the slightest intonations and inflections of voice in his characters, which give the reader almost as much information as actors would with regard to the secret meaning of their words, is practically never content with simple description, and he rarely leaves the dialogue to the reader's free interpretation. He only does so, in fact, when the apparent meaning of the spoken words exactly covers the hidden meaning. Should there be the slightest discrepancy between the conversation and the sub-conversation, should they not entirely cover each other, he immediately intervenes; at times, before the character speaks, at others, as soon as he has spoken, to show all he sees, explain all he knows; and he leaves no uncertainty except that which he himself is bound to feel, in spite of all his endeavours, his privileged position, the powerful instruments of investigation he has forged.

But these countless, tiny movements, which prepare the dialogue, are for Proust, from his point of observation, what waves and eddies on a body of water are for a cartographer who is studying a region from the air; he only sees and reproduces the broad, motionless lines that these movements compose, the points at which the lines join, cross or separate; he recognises among them those that have already been explored, and designates them by their known names: jealousy, snobbishness, fear, modesty, etc. . . .; he describes, classifies and names those he has discovered; he seeks to deduce general principles from his observations. On this vast map representing, for the most part, hardly explored regions, which he spreads out before his readers, the latter, their eyes glued to his baton with all the attention they can summon, try their best to see clearly; and they feel rewarded for their pains every time they succeed in recognising and following visually to the very end, those frequently numerous, long lines, when, like rivers that flow into the sea, they cross, separate and mingle in the mass of the dialogue.

But by appealing to the reader's voluntary attention, to his memory, by continually calling upon his faculties of comprehension and reasoning, this method foregoes at the same time everything upon which the Behaviourists, with exaggerated optimism, founded all their hopes: which is an element of freedom, of what is inexpressible, of mystery, the direct and purely sensory contact with things, which should bring into action all the reader's instinctive faculties, the resources of his unconscious, and his divinatory powers.

Although the results obtained by the Behaviourists through appeal to these blind forces are undoubtedly much weaker than their authors are willing to believe—even in those of their works in which the implications are richest and the sub-surface indications deepest—it is nonetheless true that they exist, and that one of the virtues of a work of fiction is to allow them also to come into play.

And yet, in spite of the rather serious charges that may be brought against analysis, it is difficult to turn from it today without turning one's back on progress.

For surely it is preferable, in spite of all obstacles and possible disappointments, to try to perfect, with a view to adapting it to fresh research, an instrument which, when it will have been further perfected by new generations, will permit them to describe more convincingly, with more truth and life, new situations and sentiments, than to fall back upon devices made to seize what today is mere appearance, to tend to strengthen more and more the natural penchant we all have for effects of illusion.

It is therefore permissible to dream—without blinding ourselves to all that separates the dream from its reality—of a technique that might succeed in plunging the reader into the stream of these subterranean dramas of which Proust only had time to obtain a rapid aerial view, and concerning which he observed and reproduced nothing but the broad motionless lines. This technique would give the reader the illusion of repeating these actions himself, in a more clearly aware, more orderly, distinct and forceful manner than he can do in life, without their losing that element of indetermination, of opacity and mystery that one's own actions always have for the one who lives them.

The dialogue, which would be merely the outcome or, at times, one of the phases of these dramas, would then, quite naturally, free itself of the conventions and restraints that were made indispensable by the methods of the traditional novel. And thus, imperceptibly, through a change of rhythm or form, which would espouse and at the same time accentuate his own sensation, the reader would become aware that the action had moved from inside to outside.

The dialogue, having become vibrant and swollen with these movements that propel and subtend it, would be as revealing as theatrical dialogue, however commonplace it might seem in appearance.

All of this, of course, being merely a matter for possible research and hope.

However, these problems, which dialogue poses more and more urgently to all novelists, whether they care to recognise it or not, have been solved, up to a certain point, only in a very different way, by an English writer who is still little known in France, Ivy Compton-Burnett.

The absolutely original solution, which has both distinction and power, that she has found for them, would suffice for her to deserve the place unanimously accorded her by English critics and by a certain portion of the English reading-public: that is, of one of the greatest novelists that England has ever had.

Indeed we cannot help admiring the discernment of both critics and public who have been able to see the novelty and importance of a work which, in many respects, is disconcerting.

For nothing could be less timely than the social groups that Ivy Compton-Burnett describes (the wealthy upper middle-class and the petty English nobility during the years 1880 to 1900); nothing could be more limited than the family circle in which her characters move, nothing more outmoded than the descriptions of their physical appearance by which she introduces them, or more astonishing than the off-handedness with which she unravels her plots, according to the most conventional methods, and the monotonous obstinacy with which, during forty years of labour, and throughout twenty books, she has posed and solved in an identical manner, the same problems.

But her books have one absolutely new feature, which is that they are nothing but one long continuation of dialogues. Here again, the author presents them in the traditional manner, holding herself aloof, very ceremoniously aloof, from her characters, and limiting herself as a rule, just as the Behaviourists do, to simply reproducing their words and quietly informing the reader, without trying to vary her formulas, by means of the monotonous 'said X,' 'said Y'.

But these dialogues, upon which everything rests, have nothing in common with the short, brisk, life-like conversations that, reduced to themselves, or accompanied by a few cursory explanations, risk reminding us more and more of the heavily circled little clouds that issue from the mouths of the figures in comic supplement drawings.

These long, stilted sentences, which are at once stiff and sinuous, do not recall any conversations we have ever heard. And yet, although they seem strange, they never give an impression of being spurious or gratuitous.

The reason for this is that they are located not in an imaginary place, but in a place that actually exists: somewhere on the fluctuating frontier that separates conversation from sub-conversation. Here the inner movements, of which the dialogue is merely the outcome and as it were the furthermost point— usually prudently tipped to allow it to come up to the surface —try to extend their action into the dialogue itself. To resist their constant pressure and contain them, the conversation stiffens, becomes stilted, it adopts a cautious, slackened pace. But it is because of this pressure that it stretches and twists into long sinuous sentences. Now a close, subtle game, which is also a savage game, takes place between the conversation and the sub-conversation.

More often than not, the inside gets the better of it: something keeps cropping out, becoming manifest, disappearing then coming back again; something that continually threatens to make everything explode.

The reader, who has remained intent, on the lookout, as though he were in the shoes of the person to whom the words are directed, mobilises all his instincts of defence, all his powers of intuition, his memory, his faculties of judgement and reasoning; there is hidden danger in these sweetish sentences, murderous impulses are creeping into affectionate solicitude, an expression of tenderness suddenly distils a subtle venom.

Occasionally, ordinary conversation appears to win the day, when it suppresses the sub-conversation too deeply. Then, often just at the moment when the reader thinks he will finally be able to relax, the author suddenly abandons her silence and intervenes to warn him briefly and without explanation, that none of what has just been said is true.

But the reader is not often tempted to depart from his attitude of vigilance. He knows that here every word is of importance. The by-words, the quotations, the metaphors, the ready-made, pompous or pedantic expressions, the platitudes, vulgarities, mannerisms and pointless remarks with which these dialogues are cleverly studded are not, as they are in ordinary novels, distinctive signs that the author pins on the characters to make them more easily recognisable, more familiar and more 'alive'. They are here, one feels, what they are in reality: the resultant of numerous entangled movements, that have come up from the depths, and which anyone perceiving them from the outside takes in at a glance, but which he has neither the time nor the means to separate and name.

No doubt this method is content to make the reader constantly suspect the existence, the complexity and the variety of the inner movements. It does not make him acquainted with them, in the way that techniques which plunged him into their depths and made him navigate through their currents, could succeed in doing. But it has at least the superiority over these latter techniques of having immediately attained to perfection. And by so doing it has succeeded in giving to traditional dialogue the worst blow it has received so far.

Quite obviously, one day in the near future, this one along with all the others, will seem incapable of describing anything but appearances. And nothing could be more cheering and more stimulating than this thought. It will be the sign that all is for the best, that life goes on, and that we must not turn back, but strive to go farther forward.

Nouvelle Revue Française, January-February 1956. Translated by Maria Jolas for *Tropisms and the Age of Suspicion*, Calder & Boyars, London, 1963; George Braziller Inc., New York, 1963.

Charles Burkhart

I. COMPTON-BURNETT: THE SHAPE OF A CAREER

SOME LIVES HAVE a shape to them, though more often in fiction than in 'real life'. They are very rare. They have a beginning, a middle, and of course an end, and all their parts contribute to a significant pattern, so that an observer can stand back from the completed design of such a life when it is over and say, This is what it was like. Many a biography attempts to impose too simple a shape; on the other hand most people, including fictional characters, seem to be struck more frequently by the lack of pattern or meaningful immersion in life than by its presence, and could say with Ionesco's Bérenger, early in *Rhinoceros*: 'Moi je ne m'y fais pas. Non, je ne m'y fais pas, à la vie'; or with Chekhov's ancient Firs, at the end of *The Cherry Orchard*: 'Life has slipped past me just as though I hadn't lived.'

I think that Ivy Compton-Burnett's life was one of the rare ones with a shape to it. Perhaps her biographers will help us to see it; in the meantime her twenty novels supply some evidence. An attempt to understand a novel is also an attempt to understand the mind and personality (the basic data of biography) behind it, since novels are not written by computers (and in passing one can point out that curiosity is a passionate trait of innumerable Compton-Burnett characters). Of course it is what the novels are like that counts most and comes first; yet I think that an attempt to discern the direction of her career in art must keep in touch with the directional elements of the life behind it which the art in some way embodies.

It is an interesting attempt because of the widespread notion that all her novels are identical. It's a notion to which one of her characters contributes, a witty lady named Charity Marcon in *Daughters and Sons*: 'Books are very like plants. They are better, the more they are weeded, and they come up out of each other and are all the same.' Who can keep all twenty of the novels straight? It's easy to remember that Fagin is in *Oliver Twist*,

Micawber in *David Copperfield*, and Bella Wilfer in *Our Mutual Friend*, but how many Compton-Burnett experts can say in which three of her novels these three wonderful cooks appear: Mrs Spruce, Mrs Frost, and Mrs Selden? The titles of the books are so alike; after a slow start, and a slowing down at the end, they came out at such regular intervals; within the books the conventions are as severe as in any other classical artist: the novels are ninety per cent dialogue, concern power, secrets, jealousy, illegitimacy, incest, money, and death, take place in a late-Victorian or Edwardian house in the country, have a tyrant, a choric and inquisitive neighbouring family, and a plot whose external features are the detritus of Victorian melodrama used with almost contemptuous arbitrariness (lost and stolen documents, overheard conversations, shipwrecked thought-dead characters who reappear)—but whose internal feature may be a strong and organic image which the title itself often suggests (*Two Worlds and Their Ways, Darkness and Day, The Present and the Past*). It is true that her books are more alike one another than those of any other great writer, but I do not see how this can be called a defect, as it sometimes has been: they stand one after the other in their own brilliant integrity, their glittering intelligence, insight, and wit. The as yet unattempted thing is not just to make distinctions among them but to ascertain the figure in the carpet, the rhythm of her life as a writer from the clumsy beginning (*Dolores*, 1911) to the thin and brittle ending (*The Last and the First*, published posthumously in 1971); the increasing richness culminating in the prime of life, prime of creativity, with her masterpiece *Manservant and Maidservant* (1947).

The rise and fall in her career can be generalised with various terms. It can be called from crudity to accomplishment to aridity; from conservatism to conventions to echoes of conventions; from tragic wit to comedy to bitter comedy; from in-turning to expansiveness to the solipsistic; from raw energy to total creativity to five-finger exercise. It is best to begin with the first and the last.

Dolores is all influence, and the influence is that of George Eliot. It is about duty, self-sacrifice, suffering, and other moral considerations. The voice of the novel is elaborate, clogged, and confusing; she hadn't found her own voice well enough to sound simple. Oddities of diction and syntax, wit that smoulders not glitters, heavy attempts at psychoanalysis in the style of Eliot, a narrative moving in fits and starts, the most tiresome of heroines: this is how *Dolores* is amateur. Foreshadowings exist— in dialogue, of wit; in action, of sibling rivalry; in characters, of sophisticates and fools—but the vision is tentative, echoes obfuscate, uncertainties betray the unpractised hand. The degree to which her brother helped her or himself wrote this novel cannot be determined, but whatever the causes of the conflicting intentions and varieties of tone, they awaited resolution for over ten years (*Pastors and Masters*, her first 'real' novel, did not appear until 1925), as if she must find herself, by herself alone. The nineteen books that succeed *Dolores* are not a development of an early allegiance to, so much as a reaction against George Eliot. Like every writer, she began as 'influenced'; she achieved her own tone quicker than most.

Whatever the dry and compulsive quality of *The Last and the First*, published just half a century after *Dolores*, it is entirely her own. This novel sounds as if we were already beginning to hear her at a distance, as if she were receding into literature. It is the work of a very old woman, of fitful power; it is very short, and shadowy. It is like the skeleton of one of the big novels of her central period; it sketches the familiar two households, which here include an ageing female power figure at war with a fledgling tyrant, her stepdaughter; a butler of suave and pompous diction; a foolish young man given to fulsome rhetoric; pathetically suppressed children whose recourse is wit. Money wins the day for the younger tyrant, but the battlelines are blurred; issues are raised only to be instantly resolved. There are no false steps (*Dolores* is a maze of them), but there aren't very many steps of any kind. It is a posthumous work and sounds like one.

To go back to the beginning, to the novel which finally succeeded *Dolores*, *Pastors and Masters* of 1925 is also a short work. A war had intervened between it and *Dolores*; if *Dolores* was written by a young woman brought up in a Victorian household and concerned Victorian concepts like duty, *Pastors and Masters* is, in terms of thought, at least a generation later.

Chicanery—here to do with a purloined manuscript—informs what appears to be the most respectable conduct, as if all the skeletons locked in Victorian cupboards were making a rattling entrance; no one is punished, because a moral realism has replaced a moral idealism; pretence, foolishness, and duplicity abound. But the tone is mild, light, and charming. There is a tyrant; if only a preliminary sketch, the Reverend Henry Bentley is truly malignant. But there is also the first of those witty sophisticates whose high frivolity is superbly moral, intelligent, and impotent. Her name is Emily Herrick, sister of the proprietor of a boys' school:

> 'This is a good room to come back to,' said Herrick. 'That hall and the woman, and poor Merry shuffling up to do his duty! It made me shiver.'
> 'The sight of duty does make one shiver,' said Miss Herrick. 'The actual doing of it would kill one, I think.'

The exhilaratingly light, quick sentences of her dialogue of wit have begun, total contrast to the typical style of *Dolores*, heavy and convoluted as it is. *Pastors and Masters* is set in a boys' school and *Dolores* is largely set in a girls' school (schools are also used as settings in three later novels—*More Women than Men*, *Two Worlds and Their Ways*, and *The Last and the First*), but the setting is not in itself meaningful or thematic, as it might be in Dickens or George Eliot; Miss Burke, a shrewd woman in *Mother and Son*, 'had learned that the setting of human experience was no key to itself.'

Just the length of the novels is a signpost. It gradually increases until the major works of the middle period are roughly of the same size—substantial, but not what one would call long books—*Elders and Betters* (1944), *Manservant and Maidservant* (1947), *Two Worlds and Their Ways* (1949), *Darkness and Day* (1951); and then the length gradually decreases, until the last two or three novels are once again as short as was *Pastors and Masters*. The novel which followed is her first true success—*Brothers and Sisters* (1929); it is longer, less episodic, altogether more realised.

What happened with *Brothers and Sisters* is that she tapped

F

the tragic vein. Throughout this book the word 'tragedy' is insistently and self-consciously employed. In its tragic heroine, Sophia Stace, who is married to her brother, she created a tyrant which no later hero or heroine surpasses in authority and interest. The invocation of Greek themes and situations fully released the Compton-Burnett wit; her unique blend of comedy and tragedy has now been attained. Another paradox is that it was a return to basic obsessional events of her younger life (which the plot of this novel stylises) that, as an artist, released her. She found her style, because she found herself. The time of *Pastors and Masters* is roughly contemporary with its writing, but *Brothers and Sisters* goes back some two or three decades to the time of her girl-hood or young womanhood, and this is to be the period of all the remainder of her novels. She shows family life at its most intense just at the point in time when the family as a viable social unit was breaking down, along with a great deal else.

What happened when it became too intense is shown again in the story of Harriet Haslam in the following novel, *Men and Wives*. The author was now at home with her themes. Harriet's son Matthew ends by poisoning her. In her love and irritability, her sleeplessness and insistence, Harriet is a contrast to Sophia Stace's vigour, self-importance, and manner of coupling com-mand and endearment. Harriet's story is almost too grim and ironic, in that it takes her death to accomplish her aims—each of her four children comes to follow the lines in marriage or career that she had tried, when alive, to lay down for them. In the end, after her end, she is all-powerful. Her creator must have recog-nised from *Brothers and Sisters* where her creativity could lead her, the dark geography of her genius. Because there are signs of flowering and fulfilment everywhere, of range triumphantly extended. There are twenty or so important characters, each unfalteringly defined; there is a superb study of sexuality in the woman Matthew loves, Camilla Christy; servants—who will become increasingly important—now appear in the snobbish and severe butler with the splendid name of Buttermere; there are the hypocritical and fake and meretricious seen in cold comedy. Almost the only warmth is that of Lady Hardisty, Harriet's elderly friend, whose wit, gleaming among the grimness, seems to rescue her and us from hopelessness. It is a very dark book, and the next, *More Women than Men*, is both lighter and more light-weight, a return to laughter. Set in a girls' school governed by a less attractive tyrant than either Sophia or Harriet, the murderous Josephine Napier, *More Women than Men* is a very sexual book, where the men and women are attracted both to women and to men—it seems as if it's the attraction that counts, and gender is secondary. In Miss Munday, a senior teacher at the school and drollest of ladies, there is sheer comedy, while in Felix Bacon, who goes comfortably from man to woman, there is sheer wit, though not for this reason.

It is not as effective a novel as its predecessor *Men and Wives* or its successor *A House and Its Head* because it is a little diffuse; and because it only approximates the compulsive archetype, a single family under the sway of a tyrant. In *A House and Its Head* the tyrant is male. I do not agree with Edward Sackville-West who said that Compton-Burnett men are never masculine men; I think that she is one of the few novelists whose own sex is no hindrance in creating what's called the opposite. In *A Room of One's Own* Virginia Woolf said that 'It is fatal for any one who writes to think of their sex. It is fatal to be a man or woman pure and simple; one must be woman-manly or man-womanly.' A prescription that Ivy fulfilled better than Virginia, perhaps. (In passing, one remembers that the Hogarth Press refused publication of *Brothers and Sisters*.)

Not only in the male tyrant, Duncan Edgeworth, but in other ways the strategies are more fertile, the areas claimed both more cultivated and more broad. Duncan is the first treatment of the tyrant as god, a theme less metaphysical than it at first sounds. Tyrants, like God, are omnipotent, omnipresent, omniscient— the latter two traits serving the former, in that God knows everything because he overhears all conversations, and uses this knowledge for his alert despotism. The plot is by now patently preposterous on the surface—e.g. a child whose illegitimacy is obvious because he inherits a white lock of hair from his real not his putative father; though the structure underneath, the three marriages of Duncan, is solid and satisfying. By now there are characters in great variety and profusion, the splendid comic member among them being Dulcia Bode, who has a passion for older spinsters and for clichés:

> 'Miss Fellowes!' cried Dulcia, bounding after Beatrice; 'I am going to do it. I have screwed my courage to the pitch. Turn and rend me if you must; I am going to take the plunge. May I call you by your Christian name? There, it is out!'

This novel is so richly peopled that one may fail to observe some of its themes. For instance, attacks on religion are made both in the remarks of the atheist clergyman Oscar Jekyll, and in the fraudulent piety of ladies such as Beatrice Fellowes. On the other hand the novels have by now dispensed ruthlessly with transitions between scenes, any but nominal descriptions of setting, any but formal descriptions of characters. Everything is dialogue. We are told of one minor character—Beatrice Fellowes again—that her inner life was 'as much concealed as other people's,' and we are spared the conventional psychological analysis of the 1920's or '30's English novel: dialogue, in short, is an external method that, through its *'sous-conversation'*, as Nathalie Sarraute calls it, tells us what is going on inside.

It is one way in which these novels are modern, not transitional, not Victorian. Another modern aspect, not quite unrelated I think, is the insistence on objects as objects, the existential gap posited between man and thing: the portrait of Duncan Edgeworth's first wife in *A House and Its Head*, the manuscript in *Pastors and Masters*, the earrings in *Two Worlds and Their Ways*. These objects seem to assume a life of their own but not a human life. As she relies more and more on dialogue, less and less on authorial comment, she seems to occupy the solipsistic stage, the mental arena, of Beckett. The less we are directly told of what her people are thinking, the more, through the ever-increasing suggestiveness of their speech, we indirectly know. Also like Beckett, obviously, is her fusion of tragedy and comedy. Like him too is a 'game' quality, a 'set-piece' quality to situations in which the combatants are locked in airy verbal combat or debate. It could be said that the arbitrariness of her plots is an historical reflection of the breakdown in the belief in causality, which operates deterministically in most Victorian writers (especially George Eliot and Hardy). As for morality, poetic injustice has replaced poetic justice, and here again she is like Beckett, where sudden cruelty abounds, and is unpunished. Unlike Beckett are her stoicism and her invulnerability. As in the work of many a modern artist, the surrealistic is always hovering at the edge of her novels—in the magic realism of the object, already described; in the dreamlike, mythic, and amoral intensity of her people's desires; in the unpunished and unpunishable theft or incest or murder.

The next three novels, which conclude what I would call her early period, continue to extend her scope. *Daughters and Sons* (1937) is one of her funniest novels, and one of the reasons is that children now join the cast of characters. Muriel Ponsonby— like all Compton-Burnett children, and most Compton-Burnett adults—is extremely intelligent, and has the real oddity, precocity, shyness, suddenness of a very bright child. She is seventy or eighty years younger than her tyrannical grandmother, Sabine Ponsonby, who attacks her and everyone else with an aged virulence un-matched for elegance in the earlier tyrants. Money now becomes all-important—there is never quite enough of it—and is to remain so in every novel to the end; parsimony is now added to the portrait of the tyrant. Money has become the chief means to power, and wills are influenced, changed, burned, with a sort of economic gusto. The title of the next novel is *A Family and a Fortune* (1939). People think more, not less, about money, as they get older.

A Family and a Fortune is bolder than ever. There is no harsher personage in the novels than Matty Seaton in this work, yet she can be convincingly kind; the portrait of her nephew Dudley, ~~Aubrey~~ a sensitive and physically handicapped adolescent boy who is ruefully self-mocking, self-protecting, is immensely touching; while more tragic than touching is the desperate flight through the snow of Dudley, a weak and gentle man, with Matty's cruelly mistreated companion, Miss Griffin. The powerful study of the illness and death of Matty's sister Blanche, wife to the chief tyrant, Edgar, is balanced by Dudley's near-fatal illness which is followed by an as-if-mythic rebirth. The emotional centre of the novel is Dudley's and his selfish brother Edgar's love for each other.

The Compton-Burnett family swells to the size of an army in *Parents and Children* (1941), where there are nine children. Each of the nine is so engaging in his own way, especially the three-year-old Nevill with his autocratic habit of speaking of himself in the third person, that we may slight the interest of their elders, though perhaps not of the superb comic creation Bertha Mullet, a nursemaid with delusions of past grandeur which she embroiders into tales for the younger children. This novel says less about the struggle for power in a family than it says about the family itself, which gives it a kind of sociological and historical value.

Bertha is a portent of what is common to the first two middle novels, *Elders and Betters* (1944) and *Manservant and Maidservant* (1947), a more open and robust humour. The author is in full stride, vigorous with creative energy; dark wit persists, but now the comedy of character triumphs. Her people have become more diverse, and less easily categorised as good or bad. Moral observation is even more trenchant and daring; Anna Donne, the chief wrongdoer in *Elders and Betters*, a liar who misappropriates an inheritance from one aunt and drives another to suicide, goes unpunished. There are wonderful set-pieces in this novel, like the scene of thirteen assembled at the luncheon table in Chapter VI, where superstition keeps all thirteen standing for page after page. Never were lesbian lovers in real or imagined life as funny as Ethel and Cook in this novel. Most of the inhabitants of Compton-Burnett's servant world have the superiority complex of inferiors; many of the other hired dependants—nursemaids, governesses, companions—are kindly, dependable, and unassertive, which may be the reason for, as well as the badge of, their dependency.

The brighter side becomes brilliant in *Manservant and Maidservant*. Horace Lamb, father and tyrant, barely escapes assassination a time or two, but the incidents are too preposterously plotted to bother with. What matters is the goodness of his wife and brother, the humanity of his children, and the glorious comedy of the servants' hall, where Bullivant the butler holds forth, Mrs Selden the cook sings her chapel hymns, and Bartle the boy footman and Miriam the round red scullery maid are variously suppressed and patronised. The novel ends on an odd happy note: Miss Buchanan, a taciturn but humorous woman who keeps a shop in the village, has been discovered to be illiterate, and Miriam is to teach her to read. It is impossible to indicate the verve and variety of these and the rest of the characters, of the impetus and conviction of the dialogue, of the sense one gets of a fully employed creativity: such a quality as can be seen more readily in the work of a painter who has attained complete competence in his craft, or the performance of a great musician or a star dancer. *Manservant and Maidservant* is her most compassionate work, and in a sense her most serene.

Two Worlds and Their Ways is a falling off from joy, but has perhaps the best structure of the novels. There are only seven very long chapters, each of which is a large and logical development of the theme; for example, there are parallel chapters devoted to the school career of Clemence Shelley and her brother Sefton; both cheat, are caught, and are publicly exposed. Further chapters show that their elders are no better. Their mother is a thief, their father and grandfather have fathered bastards, their half-brother Oliver has an incestuous homosexual affair with his nephew, also named Oliver; yet all these wrongdoers are far more attractive people in their carefully sorted-out wrongdoings than the headmistress of Clemence's school, Clemence's mean-spirited, priggish, and grasping aunt who has only her name—Lesbia Firebrace—to recommend her.

By 1951, when *Darkness and Day* was published, Ivy Compton-Burnett was an old woman, and in her novels it begins to be seen that she was. If her first two huge subjects were power and money, a third is now added: death. Around this time died her friend of many years, the well-known historian of the decorative arts, Margaret Jourdain. *Darkness and Day* develops old themes. The mistaken belief (the darkness) which Edmund and Bridget Lovat share, that they are father and daughter as well as husband and wife, is dispelled, by the light, or day, of knowledge; but we do not pay as much attention to Edmund and Bridget as we do to the aged Sir Ransom Chace, who is eighty-eight, or Selina Lovat, who is seventy-eight, both of whom may be masterfully witty and keen but who know they are soon to die, in the course of things which is called natural but whose unnaturalness they insistently point out. There is more generalisation about life or death; sentences are shorter and sometimes cryptic; and a reader must be still more alert, since there are pages of dialogue where speakers' names are barely mentioned. The abstract statement, depending particularly on floating pronouns, has increased, and will continue to do so. Occasionally a certain aridity is felt. There are highly comic servants, fiendishly intractable children, sharp and significant references to Greek tragedy, all of which show that the hand had not lost its cunning. But now it was old.

Shorter, perhaps slighter, but not without surprises is *The Present and the Past* (1953). If *Darkness and Day* is the borderline work between middle and late, *The Present and the Past* is clearly the latter. It begins with one of those surrealistic scenes in which the children in the novels sometimes figure, like the Calderon children's worship of their gods Chung and Sung-Li in *Elders and Betters*; here it is the sickness of a hen, whose death is being accelerated by other hens pecking it, to the fascination of the three-year-old Toby and his brother and sister. Later Toby conducts a funeral service for a dead mole.

There is no melodrama, coincidence, or creakiness of plot in *The Present and the Past*; it has a realistic and believable story line of a tyrant whose first and second wives come to like each other better than they like him and come to disregard him to the extent that he has to fake a suicide attempt to regain the limelight. His cheat discovered, he is once again found ill, this time genuinely so, but family and servants, refusing to be tricked twice, ignore him, and he dies. The novel trails off, rather than ending. There may be fine moments as when the boy Fabian, who is thirteen, says, 'My life was over when I was four. I wonder how many people can say that.' But perspectives are generally flatter, as in the character of old Mr Clare, grandfather to the children— never described, no more than a witty voice occasionally heard.

There is still enough craft and compulsion to fuel a recovery, and *Mother and Son* (1955) is that. Miranda Hume is one of the pure power figures, possessing a kind of chastity of naked will, and outspoken as a god ('There is nothing I cannot say,' she says;

and says it). Excessive filial attachment, though this side of incestuous, reappears, as the title forewarns, in the devotion of Miranda's son Rosebery to her. A pompous and foolish but likeable man, Rosebery is left by his mother's death 'partnerless', as the last words in the novel say. Although both he and Miranda's husband propose marriage to other women after her death, nothing comes of their efforts (it is habit, not metaphysic, that insures a tyrant's continued sway even after he or she is gone). Someone says, 'A great deal goes on beneath the surface in a family,' and *Mother and Son* once again shows it, with the old candour and accuracy. It is one of the simpler novels, but has a strength of its own.

How conscious or thoughtful or deliberate actually was the curtailment of range? Probably very little. In any case *A Father and His Fate* in 1957 continues it. This novel is entirely organised around Miles Mowbray, one of the most successful of the tyrants. When Miles's wife is believed lost at sea, he decides to marry his adopted heir's fiancée, continues with the plan even when he learns his wife is still alive, and rationalises his conduct strongly when it is discovered. He suffers no lasting losses. The economy of this novel is particularly effective in that every other character serves as witness and chorus to the deeds of Miles, who is prime mover, arbiter, once again like the gods amoral. But the novel is bleaker. The earlier delight in silliness has evanesced. Moreover the dialogue of wit disappears altogether from some pages, with only a tight rational exchange to replace it, which sometimes seems to run a subject into the ground, and bury it, and which does not comment upon itself, authorial asides now barely existing. It is also bleaker because there are no children, and only, for servants, a very brief butler. Every *sotto voce* remark is now automatically overheard, every event in the main household is immediately followed by a visit *en masse* from members of the subordinate household, and, in short, there is an insistence on conventions that before were more scrupulously spaced.

A Heritage and Its History (1959) follows the same strategy of curtailing, of centralising the focus. The heritage is the estate of the Challoner family and the history is Simon Challoner's love for it; and his final attainment of it, after vicissitudes. Because the author is now a very old woman, her characters talk about death, almost as if it could help, in lines that can sound like the ancient wise Oedipus at Colonus: 'To live is nothing but wishing. It is always too late.' Or:

> 'Young people forget the gains of experience,' said Julia. 'If we went back to youth, we should give up a great deal.'
>
> 'What would it be?' said Simon. 'What exactly are the gains?'
>
> 'An insight into motive,' said Sir Edwin, 'a habit of expecting little, an estimate of what is much. Acceptance of fading away, and of other people's acceptance of it.'

In themselves stoic and strong, there are too many of such passages, too many sudden marriages, illegitimacies, and deaths for so short a work. The proportion of melodramatic speech to speech of wit or comedy is much higher now, which is a sign of strain, like a singer who can only sing his high notes loud. It is dark indeed; the creeper which enshrouds the house—the heritage—at the beginning of the story is still there at the end, years and years later. In these last novels all the households are even more pressingly short of money, the land bringing in so much less than it did. If Simon Challoner's efforts to retain his heritage intact go against the thrust of history, they seem, because he is not a really attractive figure, more stubborn than heroic. The young children Claud and Emma are the only bright spots in this gloomy tale.

Still another male tyrant dominates the following novel, Ninian Middleton of *The Mighty and Their Fall* (1961). Like his predecessors, he may fall, but, again like them, he suffers no damage. A more basic subject is the love between Ninian and his daughter. Both are guilty of misdeeds—he attempts to destroy a will in her favour, she attempts to hide a letter from a woman which accepts Ninian's proposal of marriage; both are found out, neither pays the consequences, and their relationship is closer at the end than it was at the beginning. Compared with its immediate predecessor, this is a tighter, funnier, and less melodramatic book, a rhythmic recovery of inspiration.

A God and His Gifts (1963) is an apotheosis novel, in which sense it can be considered her last work. It is her most personal book in that its tyrant, Hereward Egerton, is a writer, and he is as God. So great a force is his creativity that it spills over from his books and he dominates everyone he meets; it takes a directly sexual form and he spawns offspring everywhere, leaving behind him a tangled trail of illegitimacies. No hungry generations will tread him down, for he will seduce his sons' wives. A fecund and popular writer, he has 'brought joy to thousands'; although his father and his butler may think writing novels unfit occupation for a gentleman, he is superbly beyond their and any criticism, and can eloquently say that he is. Union of art and sexuality, he is not evil or vicious or harsh or deceptive like tyrants in the earlier novels; instead he is amoral or pre-moral, at once primitive and grand.

There was to be another novel, *The Last and the First*, published after her death, but it is a coda, and *A God and His Gifts* brings her career into a shapely and formal consistency. The wide and debatable claims made for the artist in this testamentary and penultimate novel have as one of their best arguments the eighteen novels which preceded it. It is a career with unique integrity of intention, and nearly unique authority of vision.

John Ginger

IVY COMPTON-BURNETT

W HEN THE TYRANNICAL Duncan returns home unexpectedly in Ivy Compton-Burnett's *A House and Its Head*, his daughter warns the family of his approach: ' "My father is come!" quoted Nance. "He is in the hall at the moment." ' The allusion (one hasn't the temerity to add *of course*) is to *Mansfield Park* and to Sir Thomas Bertram who, having just returned from Antigua, walks through his study door and finds himself 'on the stage of a theatre, and opposed to a ranting young man, who appeared likely to knock him down backwards'.

Ivy Compton-Burnett's characters are allowed virtually no small-talk. Literature is an exception. Very occasionally, Shakespeare or George Eliot are discussed—usually when guests are present; and in *Pastors and Masters* (1925) Jane Austen is mentioned. Francis has no time for 'books by ladies for ladies', and for once the feminist Miss Basden is in agreement with him: 'I can't get over the littleness in her books.' One of the striking features of Ivy Compton-Burnett's own literary career was her ability to send critics scurrying for comparisons. Euripides has been mentioned; and on the dust-jacket of my copy of *Men and Wives*, Edward Sackville-West talks about Henry James while Edwin Muir cites Congreve. (Surely, Oscar Wilde also deserves a mention?)

There is some justification for following the lead we were given in that rather recondite cross-reference. Ivy Compton-Burnett's characters are drawn from the same class as Jane Austen's and seem to be just as socially insulated in their turn-of-the-century settings as the inhabitants of Longbourn or Hartfield. There is the same implied geography: a big house, a lodge, a vicarage and, at most, one or two other residences on a shadowy perimeter. Intrusions in the form of visits or unexpected letters provide the main impetus for the plot, and the action is unfolded during the course of meals and social calls. Sometimes the debt to Jane

Austen is acknowledged stylistically, as in *Men and Wives* (1931) when we are told that Mrs Christy 'suspected she had a remarkable brain, and found that her spontaneous conversation proved it beyond her hopes.'

Perhaps, if Jane Austen had stopped short of *Mansfield Park*, it would have been possible to regard her and the creator of Mrs Christy as altogether kindred spirits. But Ivy Compton-Burnett must surely have regarded this last novel as a betrayal of the enlightened eighteenth-century principles that *Emma* and *Pride and Prejudice* had acknowledged. Long before Duncan interrupts the tea-party, we have written him off as a tyrant. Sir Thomas, arriving in the nick of time to spare Fanny Price the agony of standing-in at a rehearsal of *Lovers' Vows*, is an equally awe-inspiring father, but he has the author on his side. The Crawfords, who have lured the Bertram family into amateur theatricals, are amusing but morally suspect. Wilberforce and Hannah More are standing in the wings. The evangelical revival is directing uncomfortable blasts towards Mansfield Rectory, and Fanny, the last and least characteristic of the heroines, will become the wife of a parson who takes his duties seriously. Surely, Dame Ivy couldn't have approved?

It is the active irreligiousness of her books, as much as their materially comfortable and secure background, that sets them down so squarely in the Edwardian period. Unless it states otherwise, contemporary literature assumes the absence of religious belief ('Jesus' having become the great five-letter word of American literature) but the members of this society inhabit the ruins of an evangelical cult and are still on occasions threatened by it. It is always the cruder form of evangelism that intrudes in the shape of grotesques like the retired missionary, Rosamund Burtenshaw in *A House and Its Head*, who calls to proclaim the 'message of Christmas' or to make a death-bed visitation. Often to their own amusement, characters have names like Reuben, Faith, Gideon and Charity. Many are adept at quoting scripture—though not usually in the intended sense; and family prayers are found useful, if only as an instrument of domestic tyranny. There is sometimes a faint whiff of Calvinism in the air.

No self-respecting person in a Compton-Burnett novel allows

his integrity to be compromisd by any of this, though great vigilance—particularly in the case of the dying—is needed. Death is treated with a wide-eyed, almost fascinated respect (there are some memorable scenes), and more than one character steels herself against the temptation of a last-minute access of faith. 'I don't feel I am going to meet my Maker,' says Selena in *The Mighty and Their Fall* (1961). 'And if I were, I should not fear him. He has not earned the feeling. I almost think he ought to fear me.' (Ivy Compton-Burnett must have approved of St Teresa's:

'It isn't surprising you have so few friends, Lord, if this is how you treat them!')

All the sympathetic characters share Selena's agnosticism:

'She goes to church,' said Muriel. 'And she does not have to go, does she?'

'If she were religious, she would not go,' said France. 'She would have thought about her religion and lost it.'

In *A Family and a Fortune* (1939) there is a certain wistfulness over the loss of faith in an exchange that follows the death of Blanche, the mother of the family. Her father's allusion to an after-life is greeted with a mixture of awe and nervous jocularity ('they had no grasp of the mental background of his youth'):

'Boys dear,' said Justine, 'isn't this rather cheap jesting upon subjects which are serious to many people? Do you know, at this moment I could find it in me to envy Grandpa his faith?'
'We should like to have some comfort,' said Aubrey, his grin extending into the grimace of weeping, as he found himself speaking the truth.

Indirectly, the conviction that religion is a dangerous delusion, a refuge for the weak for whom reality is too stark, or a weapon for the strong who pad out their egoism or enslave others with it, seems to have been one of the principal motives that caused

eighteen remarkable books to be written between the mid-
'twenties and the mid-'sixties. 'Without a moral standard', Dame
Ivy wrote to me in 1964, 'there could be no civilized life.' But
where was this moral standard to be found? Incessantly her
characters hold up for scrutiny and analyse every remark uttered
—never casually—at breakfast, lunch or dinner, trying to find an
answer to that question. Where does cant end and truth begin?
and *what is truth*? as she frequently echoes. How much Christian
philosophy can be thrown overboard with Christian dogma?
Such basic assumptions as the possibility of being generous, or of
forgiving, or of the moral value of courage or endurance or self-
sacrifice are constantly challenged. Slipshod thinking and any form
of dishonesty (either with oneself or with others) are the capital
crimes in this world. An unwritten law requires all characters to
speak the truth to the best of their ability. (Even the 'villains'
conform to this demand, though the essential feature of an Ivy
Compton-Burnett villain is a lack of self-knowledge; and a
further complication is their tendency to use their incomplete and
badly-motivated candour against their victims.) It is all very
invigorating and ruthless and uncomfortable.

But there is a fundamental and unchanging irony in these books.
While men, women and children are granted, almost without
exception, a control over words which is rarely encountered
outside poetic drama, they find themselves in situations which are
quite beyond their control. They are dependent on neurotics or on
a past which has always been bundled rather carelessly out of
sight; they succumb to the temptation to relieve intolerable
pressures by witholding messages or destroying wills; and they are
often defenceless before the desire for sexual or emotional fulfilment. There is a permanent tension between what is natural and
what is civilised. The tyrants exult in an unashamed display of
nature: that is a clearly recognised danger. But there is a more
insidious temptation: to opt for a plaster-cast civilisation, and
allow truth (which may seem to err dangerously on the side of
nature) to receive a protective coating of cant. The sympathetic
characters find themselves uneasily situated midway between these
poles of attraction.

The theme of Ivy Compton-Burnett's first novel, *Dolores*

(1911) was self-sacrifice. After a gap of fourteen years, the great
series of dialogue novels began with *Pastors and Masters*, published
when she was forty-one. *Dolores* appears to have been disowned;
but the self-sacrifice which it portrayed in a noble light was to
recur as a theme in many later books. In *Men and Wives*, when the
Haslam children question the lawyer, Dominic Spong, about his
work, they are shocked by his airy reference to 'sacrifice of self':

'Isn't it very dreadul to see sacrifice of self?' said Griselda.
'Miss Griselda, sometimes very beautiful.'
'It seems rather ruthless to be a satisfied spectator,' said Jermyn.

Six years later, in *Daughters and Sons*, one of her finest books, she
developed this into a major theme. The central figure in its plot
is a successful novelist, John Ponsonby, who appears to be sacrific-
ing the books he would like to have written in order to produce
the best-sellers that support his large family. He is a gentle and
apparently tractable person, but the real sacrifices in this story are
not his but those of three women, his sister, his daughter and the
woman he later marries, whose love of him make them easy
material for exploitation. (For all its wit and humour, this is a
stark world.) Hetta works as unpaid secretary-cum-housekeeper
for her widowed brother and finds emotional satisfaction in the
power and sense of purpose this gives her. France, the daughter,
writes a novel and gains an unexpected insight into her father's
jealous nature when she shows him her manuscript; it is sub-
sequently published and wins a prize, and the money is surrend-
ered anonymously to John to help him out of a financial difficulty.
Up to a point, Edith, the new governess who is the real heroine of
the book, preserves her detachment from this situation, skilfully
navigating the unpredictable currents that have made life difficult
for her predecessors. But a letter finds its way into the wrong
hands, inferences are drawn, and when John is informed by his
mother that Edith is the anonymous benefactor he marries her.
Hetta discovers the truth and after a pathetic failure to demon-
strate her own indispensability by pretending to drown herself
she makes it public knowledge. Disaster is rarely unqualified in
Ivy Compton-Burnett's novels, and Hetta is allowed to escape

into marriage with the vicar (another grotesque), while John, whose callous ingratitude has sparked off the catastrophe, makes a gentlemanly profession of his satisfaction with his new marriage; but on Edith—who, with her wit and self-knowledge, has seemed to possess an impregnable strength—a sombre silence falls. The desire to be loved has made her just as vulnerable as the clumsy and passionate and more 'natural' Hetta. John's eldest daughter, the downtrodden Clare, offers her own view of family life:

> 'France is safe,' said Clare, 'and not only from the world as Father wished her to be, but from Father. And when you have to be safe from the world, it is wiser to include your family.'

Not all the personages in Ivy Compton-Burnett's novels have the strength to survive the twin onslaughts of egoism and blind fate to which she subjects them. There are many drop-outs, and those who escape the graver moral lapses may still succumb to callous facetiousness or cynicism. It is not always easy to distinguish, at first encounter, between the real cynics and those who arm themselves with a protective pseudo-cynicism. In *Daughters and Sons*, Clare is the cynic and France the realist. The distinction is clarified by events. Clare is defeated by the family situation, and her willingness to escape from it by marrying the opportunist who is advancing himself at the expense of the family reveals the depths of her cynicism:

> '. . . I want to get out of this house to another life. That is all I can think of. I have borne enough.'
> 'That is natural perhaps,' said John, turning from his daughter. 'We will leave Clare.'
> 'It is wrong and deplorable as things said to be natural always are,' said France. 'But we must leave it, as you say.'

Wisdom is usually represented by a woman in late middle-age (less often a man). She has usually had to come to terms with some deficiency: she has to work for a living; or she has peculiar looks; or she is a second wife without children of her own. While these women are often self-conscious, they also possess self-knowledge, and they use this knowledge as a defence against the egoism which may assail them from within and nearly always does threaten them from without. Their self-tolerance and humour make them gentle where the foibles of others are concerned; but they are never complacent, and their wit makes them formidable friends when unpalatable truths have to be faced. This is Rachel, in *Men and Wives*, talking to Harriet Haslam who has just invoked the ultimate deterrent of an attempted suicide against her unmanageable family:

'. . . We must take the ordinary line of reproach; nothing else would be flattering; and you do deserve flattery, Harriet, having faced death, and found it so uncongenial to face it, which makes it more heroic. You must give me a lesson in facing it, as for me it is getting imperative. I believe I shall die without facing it, and I would much rather face it without dying, as you have.'

Like her counterparts, expecting little from life and less from themselves, Rachel achieves an almost heroic stature: she shores up the collapsing edifice of family life when Harriet is at last helped to a more effective dose of poison by her son. On a lesser scale, Edith, having accidentally learned the unpleasant truth about her own situation, can attend to the trivial woes of the new governess whom everyone else is choosing to ignore. Whilst preserving their individual identities, these characters share the same scepticism, the same keen nose for insincerity and that quick tongue that can be found in action on any page indefatigably turning language inside out in the search for a moral standard that rational beings can live by. ('Being cruel to be kind is such dreadful cruelty. Being cruel to be cruel is better.')

If Ivy Compton-Burnett is to be compared to Euripides it should be less because of those acts of passion that sometimes occur between the end of one chapter and the beginning of the next (and between meals) than for the stoicism they have in common and for the moments of dark poetry: '. . . sending them forth into fear', 'She was laid away out of sight', '(her eyes) drew back into safety and silence'. The Edith Hallams and Emma Greathearts don't believe for a moment that the universe is concerned about their individual success or failure, joy or suffering; but they have faith in their own wills, and they are stylists; they pay great attention to the quality of the performance they are giving, and the maxim of Epictetus, 'In the centre of your being do not groan', seems to play an important part in the way they conduct their lives. When Stephen Marcon is introduced in *Daughters and Sons*, we seem to get the brief *credo* of that stoicism to which the author must have subscribed:

> He was a contented disappointed man, happy in his own disappointment, and seeing in his small advance in science the reward and reason of life, to which he did not assign any great reward or reason.

Perhaps Ivy Compton-Burnett's failure to call one of her novels *Father and Daughter* is a sign of her subtlety—for it is this relationship which occupies the central place in her work and which could have provided an adequate title for half-a-dozen of them. It is a theme which always spells out betrayal. In *The Mighty and Their Fall*, we find it in its bleakest form. Ninian, a widower, has a close attachment to his eldest daughter, Lavinia, but shows his failure to understand her feelings when the opportunity to remarry presents itself. The shock precipitates a moral breakdown: Lavinia hides a letter and covers her traces by allowing her grandmother to be incriminated. There is no recovery. Ninian's sanctimonious and wounding 'forgiveness' is countered by Lavinia's inability to recognise that she has done wrong. For once there is no Rachel or Edith to pick up the pieces, and cynicism is triumphant at the end of the novel when Lavinia, who has inherited some money, grudgingly allows her father the use of it, with few illusions as to the impulse behind his renewed affection.

The plot of *A Family and a Fortune* has some things in common with that of *The Mighty and Their Fall*: a re-marriage, an unexpected inheritance, a daughter who is asked to sacrifice her own feelings to a father's selfishness. But the resemblance ends there. If *The Mighty and Their Fall* is the bleakest of the novels, *A Family and a Fortune* is the warmest, and many devotees might say the best. The central figure is a woman of thirty, Justine, the eldest of the Gaveston children. In the gradual filling-out of this portrait, we see what dividends the author can draw from a technique which would appear to have many disadvantages. (We are told very little about any character directly.) Justine's personality is slowly revealed in what she says or what her family say to or about her, and our first impression is of one of those cosmic and egoistical characters we have been taught to regard with suspicion, rather than of a heroine. She is strong-minded and ebullient, and in this world her lack of subtlety appears half-way between a virtue and a comic weakness:

> 'I don't know,' said Justine. 'We might often meet a good, sound, impartial judgement.'
> 'And we know, when we have one described like that, what a dreadful judgement it is,' said her uncle.
> 'Half the truth, the blackest of lies,' said Mark.
> 'The whitest of lies really,' said Clement. 'Or there is no such thing as a white lie.'
> 'Well, there is not,' said his sister. 'Truth is truth and a lie is a lie.'
> 'What is truth?' said Aubrey. 'Has Justine told us?'

Her family is on guard. Blanche, the mother, has to ensure that her place over the coffee cups isn't usurped; her father, Edgar, is more than a little perplexed to find himself the object of so much affection. In the first half of the novel we sense a concerted effort to cut Justine down to size:

> 'Come, come, Mother, I was tactless, I admit,' said Justine. 'I know people hate confessing that they sleep in the day. I ought to have remembered it.'
> 'Justine now shows tact,' murmured Aubrey.
> 'It is possible—it seems to be possible,' said Edgar, 'to be resting with closed eyes and give the impression of sleep.'
> 'You forget the snoring, Father,' said Justine, in a voice so low and light as to escape her mother's ears.
> 'If you don't forget it too, I don't know what we are to do,' said Mark, in the same manner.
> 'Snoring is not a proof of being asleep,' said Dudley.
> 'But I was not snoring,' said Blanche, in the easier tone of one losing a grasp of a situation. 'I should have known it myself. It would not be possible to be awake and make a noise and not hear it.'
> Justine gave an arch look at anyone who would receive it. Edgar did so as a duty and rapidly withdrew his eyes as another.

But Justine's strength lies in her understanding of the people she feels compelled to organise. She is on guard against Clement's sourness, and while she recognises that the adolescent brother, Aubrey, needs her support, she seems to know in advance that he will be compelled to disown it. She is also ready to do battle with Aunt Matty, who threatens the family's equilibrium with her bid for power. Justine divines that this nice balance depends ultimately on the close relationship between Edgar and his brother, Dudley. The background to her most glaring weakness —her need not only to stage-manage the family but to be seen to do so—isn't suggested until Blanche dies, halfway through the story:

> Justine came closer and her mother saw her face.
> 'Are you my beautiful daughter?' she said, again in the rapid tone. 'The one I knew I should have? Or the other one?'
> 'I am your Justine, Mother.'
> 'Justine!' said Blanche, and threw up her arms. 'Why should we want her different?'

Blanche's death is a turning-point in the novel, for the family is threatened by change. Dudley, who has become engaged to Maria, Aunt Matty's friend, quickly finds his place taken by his brother. Aunt Matty attempts to install herself in her sister's place. The family seems to be on the point of disintegration. But now Justine's forthright leadership and her willingness to sink her own feelings for the sake of others play a crucial part in preserving harmony. We are left to infer her disillusionment when Dudley announces Edgar's engagement to Maria:

> 'Is Father's self made manifest now?' said Aubrey.
> Justine rose and shook out her skirt with a movement of discarding the traces of some pursuit.
> 'People's weaker side is not necessarily their truer self,' she said in a tone which ended the talk and enabled her uncle to leave the room.
> A silence followed his going.
> 'Are men allowed to marry someone else as soon as they like after their wives are dead?' said Aubrey.
> 'How many weeks is it?' said Mark.

'I do not know. We will not say,' said his sister. 'It can do no good.'

'It may have been the emotion of that time which prepared the way for the other.'

'It may have been. It may not. We do not know.'

'Is it often like that?' said Aubrey.

Justine sat down and drew him to her lap, and as he edged away to save her his weight, suddenly raised her hands to her head and burst into a flood of tears. Her brothers looked on in silence. Aubrey put his knee on the edge of her chair and stared before him.

'Well, that is over', she said, lifting her face. 'I had to let myself go at first. If I had not, it would only have been bottled up and broken out at some inopportune time. Witness my passages with Aunt Matty . . .'

Unlike Justine, Aunt Matty refuses at first to be reconciled to the changed balance of power, and with misplaced candour sets out to add the spice of recrimination and guilt to family life. The two women have the same temperament: both are motivated by a desire to be needed by others. But where Matty is negative and destructive, Justine, recognising the potential weakness in her own personality, forces herself into a constructive and self-effacing role: 'Pull yourselves together,' she tells her brothers, 'and remember that we are mere pawns in the game of skill and chance which is being played.'

After a series of skirmishes, she is rewarded by the sight of the family grouping themselves round her and resisting Matty's incitement to reject 'civilisation' in favour of 'nature'. For once, Justine herself is silent.

There was a pause and Matty was driven further.

'Well, it is a strange chapter that I have lived since I have been here. A strange, swift chapter. Or a succession of strange swift, chapters. If I had known what was to be, might I have been able to face it? And if not, how would it all be with us? How we can think of the might-have-beens!'

'There are no such things,' said Edgar.

'We cannot foretell the future,' said Mark. 'It might make us mould our actions differently.'

'And then how would it all be with us?' repeated Matty, in a light running tone, 'Maria not here; Justine not deposed; nothing between your father and uncle; everything so that my sister could come back at any time and find her home as she left it.'

'Is it so useful to have things ready for her return?'

'It is hardly a dependable contingency,' said Clement.

'No, no,' said Justine, with a movement of distaste, 'I am not going to join'.

'So my little flight of imagination has fallen flat.'

'What fate did it deserve?' said Edgar, in a tone which fell with its intended weight.

'Did you expect to carry us with it?' said Mark.

Matty shrank into herself, drawing her shawl about her and looking at her niece almost with appeal. The latter shook her head.

'No, no, Aunt Matty, you asked for it. I am not going to interfere.'

'What do you say to the reception of a few innocent words, Dudley?'

'I have never heard baser ones.'

Justine is Ivy Compton-Burnett's St Joan—and an altogether unlikely heroine for a novel published in 1939. It must have been tempting to leave her on the heights of her self-sacrifice; but this remarkable writer's artistry forbad that. Justine begins as a comic character, and ends as one. She slithers about on the treacherous slopes of bathos, and even when she is affirming her belief in the meaningfulness of existence (of course, it is a stoic's belief), she has to run the gauntlet of her brothers' satire:

'Uncle was heading for trouble, and at the crucial moment it came. He could not go on too long, keyed up to that pitch. The strain of the last months can only be imagined. None of us can know what it was.'

'Is Justine transfigured?' said Aubrey.

'Well, I am affected by the spectacle of intense human drama. I do not deny it.'

'It were idle to do so,' said Clement.

'It would have been better to go away at once,' said Mark, 'and not attempt the impossible.'

'I don't know,' said his sister, gazing before her. 'It was a great failure. Surely one of those that are greater than success.'

'I never quite know what those are. I suppose you mean other kinds of success. The same kind involves the same effort and has a better end.'

'And a much more convenient one,' said Clement.

'Yes, yes, more convenient,' said Justine. 'But what we have seen was surely something more than that.'

'Something quite different indeed,' said Mark.

'Surely it was worth it.'

'From our point of view as spectators?'

'Well, in the sense that all human effort must achieve something essential, even if not apparent. . . .'

Nor is she allowed a happy ending. *A Family and a Fortune* does, in fact, end gaily with Justine's call to the family to watch Edgar and Dudley, once more arm in arm, walking in the garden. But it is a happy ending only because Justine insists that it is. In the previous chapter we have been given a clear view of her changed status: Edgar is now Maria's husband, and Aubrey is beginning to transfer his always ambivalent allegiance to his step-mother:

'But Aunt Matty's loneliness and all that has happened,' said Justine, standing with her face close to the coat and bringing the lapels together. 'You do feel that you have an anchor in your children?'

Edgar turned and walked away.

'Oh, I suppose I have said the wrong thing as usual. I might have known it was hopeless to attempt to do anything for him. In my heart I did know.'

'It is good to follow the dictates of the heart,' said Clement.

'Yes, you can be supercilious. But what did you attempt after all? I did try to show Father that he had something to depend on in his home.'

'And he showed you that he could not take your view.'

'I suppose Maria has taken my place with him. Well, it would be small to mind it. I have never done much to earn the place. And it is better than her taking another. She does not feel she has taken that. We can think of that little place as open and empty, free for Mother's little shadow.'

Aubrey turned and slouched out of the room, kicking up his feet.

If the only way to prove one's devotion to Ivy Compton-Burnett is to pull a name out of a hat, perhaps one should commit oneself and say that she was the most compassionate English novelist since George Eliot.

London Magazine, January, 1970

V

THREE OBITUARIES

I

Anthony Powell

THE FIRST TIME I saw Ivy Compton-Burnett was at a party given to watch the Oxford and Cambridge Boat-race from Chiswick Mall. The setting was appropriate, because this fixture always peculiarly evokes in the mind a sense of the late nineteenth century, and the 'varsity men' of that era, rather than the undergraduates and sporting events of today. In early or later life these are the people, with their womenfolk—one uses that word advisedly—who make up the population of the Compton-Burnett novels, most of which suggest in period the years not long before the turn of the century.

Miss Compton-Burnett herself was wearing a black tricorne for the Boat-race. She looked formidably severe. I think she was severe. She saw life in the relentless terms of Greek tragedy, its cruelties, ironies, hypocrisies—above all its passions—played out against a background of triviality and ennui. Later we met on two or three occasions, but I never knew her well, and always felt the sort of constraint experienced as a child talking to an older person, who one suspected could never understand the complexities of one's own childish problems. This was absurd in a way, because we shared a lot of literary likes and dislikes (she wrote to me of Emily Brontë: 'Posterity has paid its debt to her too generously, and with too little understanding'), and we might be said to have 'got on' together very well.

I think the explanation of my sense of unease was no more and no less than what has been said; Ivy Compton-Burnett embodied in herself a quite unmodified pre-1914 personality, so that one was, in truth, meeting what one *had* encountered as a child. The particular interest and uniqueness of this is in relation to the immense individual revolutions and transformations that must, in fact, have taken place within herself, all without in the smallest degree affecting the way in which she faced the world. No writer was ever so completely of her books, and her books of her.

The Compton-Burnett novels deal with a form of life that has largely, if not entirely disappeared, though I suspect that even to this day pockets of something very similar could be found; perhaps not so much in the country, where the novels tend to be located, as in residential suburbs and seaside towns. As with all good writers, a fair amount of nonsense has been written about her subject matter, so that one hesitates to generalise for fear of adding to it, especially in these days when so many people are obsessed with the subject of 'class'.

However, let me risk suggesting that, between a still lively aristocracy merging effortlessly into an enormously proliferated middle-class, both keenly aware of what is going on round them, large gloomy moderately rich families in largish, though not immense, houses in the country, going as a matter of course to Oxford or Cambridge, interested in acquiring property or money, yet lacking almost all contact with an outer world, living in a state of almost hysterically inward-looking intensity, have become pretty rare. If we add to that the Compton-Burnett conditions that such families take little or no interest in sport, and none of the sons enter the army or navy, the field is again narrowed within the terms of reference.

This is the usual Compton-Burnett set-up, and certainly it had once had a being. My reason for thinking it not wholly extinct is partly on account of the vitality of the novels themselves—if people were ever like this, there must be people always like this; partly because one will suddenly be confronted—in a railway carriage, for example—with a great burst of overheard Compton-Burnett dialogue. However, whether or not they remain in any appreciable number, such persons form the core of the novels as they are, a social category accepted without question by the author. The men have a classical education, the women a good knowledge of standard poets. It is a 'cultivated' society, but not, one would say, an 'intellectual' one in anything like the contemporary sense. Professional writers play only a small part, artists none at all, though the children draw and paint.

The matter of 'class' is touched on here chiefly because it is almost always made such a feature by Compton-Burnett reviewers. In fact, she is not a novelist greatly concerned with class differences and nuances, as was, for example, Proust, or even Dickens. All novels must be written from a given point of view. The Compton-Burnett novels concentrate minimally on an aspect that is usually allowed undue prominence in their criticism. They are primarily concerned with human passions, and the ruthless manner in which these are usually satisfied. For an investigation of that sort, an accepted routine of manners must always be a great convenience to any novelist.

The game is played, therefore, in a manner all the players understand. Accordingly, much that is said and done is not made explicit. It might be pondered whether one of the great errors of the present day is the theory that nothing is thought to be 'true' which is not explicit; or, put another way, everything that is 'true' can be explicitly expressed. This is surely a great mistake. Life itself is not explicit. To write of it explicitly on all occasions is just as much an author's convention as any other; possibly a mistaken one. It is not, in any case, the Compton-Burnett method.

Her writing is a complete denial of any such approach. It is also, incidentally, a discommendation of a fashion of the moment, usually immature in conception, not to say half-baked, for supposedly 'showing up' the Victorians for the licence of their lives. Of course much of Victorian life was licentious. Everybody knew that at the time; only the inadequately informed are just beginning to find it out now. However, the particular social technique of that epoch was to deal with such matters obliquely. The Compton-Burnett novels show—satirically, painfully, compassionately—how that method worked out in practice.

This is not the place to argue whether or not there was more seduction, adultery, illegitimacy, incest, lesbianism, homosexuality, not to mention swindling and murder, in those days than now; above all whether there was more, or less, 'fun'. It is, however, a fact that all these subjects are dealt with in the Compton-Burnett novels in a manner, so it seems to me, unlikely to be made more effective or convincing by the recital of elaborate physical details. Nor does it seem of the smallest importance, one way or the other, that the people concerned belong on the whole to the upper-middle class; any more than that a lot of Shakespeare's plays are about kings and queens. In fact,

if I were to name a contemporary writer who suggests something
of the Compton-Burnett approach, it would be not among the
novelists, but in the plays of Harold Pinter. Mr Pinter certainly
allows himself more down-to-earth language, but conveys much
of the same ironic despair set against drearily humdrum circumstances.

Death is a subject never very far away in Ivy Compton-
Burnett's books, and, one may guess, in her imagination too.
There had been tragedies within her own family which she never
quite got over, and she could not speak of war or read a book
about it, because she had lost in war a favourite brother. Nevertheless death, like everything else, is treated by her with a sense
of proportion, an awareness that its threat is only for those who
fear it.

'Ah, my little hostess, so you are looking after us, are you?' said
Godfrey, throwing one leg over the other.

'It is so painful to me to see this house without its mistress,' said
Agatha, taking her stand by Rachel and stirring her cup. 'She is in my
mind every moment I am here. That things have to go on, and do
go on, is of course a ground for thankfulness, but their very going on
causes something very near heartache.'

'Very near,' said Rachel. 'That is an excellent way of putting it.
We are reminded that things will go on after we are dead, that people
will be happy, actually be that, when we are not anything. And yet
it would not do to have quite a heartache.'

'I suppose we ought not to feel it. We can do nothing while we
are here for those who have passed before.'

'You were thinking what we could do for them before they
passed, if we could prove we could never be happy afterwards?'

'They would not feel that, though we cannot suppress a tendency
to feel that for them,' said Agatha, and added half to herself:

'Better by far you should forget and smile,
Than that you should remember and be sad.

'I am convinced that would be—that is my dear husband's
feeling towards my life.'

'People improve so tremendously when they are dead,' said
Rachel. . . .

A final word I think she would like said. When, a long time ago, I once spoke of some novel by 'I. Compton-Burnett' to the late Roger Hinks—no less astringent as a wit and mimic than in the famed rigour of his Elgin Marbles spring-cleaning—he replied, in a tone of quiet reduction to powder that, although still unmet, I knew must be Miss Compton-Burnett's own: 'Búrnett, we call it.'

Spectator, September 6, 1969

Angus Wilson

WHEN ANY REALLY considerable writer dies, our first thought surely is for the pleasure and the illumination that his works have given us. The pleasure of Ivy Compton-Burnett's novels is easy to estimate: she made us laugh, laugh subtly, laugh a great deal, and laugh to some purpose. The illumination is harder to describe.

She made us see how the evil tyrants of this world—Matty Seaton, Horace Lamb, Josephine Napier, Duncan Edgeworth, Sir Jesse Sullivan—are all touched with finenesses, but that such finenesses can only demand our recognition, not our forgiveness of their cruelty; she made us see, too, that cruelty and tyranny built up in their sufferers many qualities of bravery, loyalty and affection—almost any of her groups of children or adolescents suffering under their tyrannical parents proved this—but she never allowed us the easy sop of saying that such happy results in the sufferers excuse for a moment those who make them suffer. As a stoic agnostic, she bade us accept a good deal with courageous indifference, without flattering ourselves that our acceptance deserved admiration, or that advertising our bravery by plucky smiling was ever more than a histrionic impertinence.

She believed that most human beings are weak, some few evil, some few others truly loving and good: but if her judgments were firm they were far from doctrinaire—humour, which she loved, could mark some of her grimmest, most dislikable characters; silliness, which she detested, she also knew could be the mark of the gentle and generous. In the age of the concentration camp, when, from 1935 or so to 1947, she wrote her very best novels, no writer did more to illumine the springs of human cruelty, suffering and bravery. Never leaving her anonymous world of one or two big houses in a late Victorian village (save for the odd private school), she contrived to be the most penetrating critic of the darkness and light of her own time.

Of course, in making bourgeois family tyranny the centre of

her world, she was the heir of the English tradition of the novel—from Richardson's Harlowe family, through Jane Austen's Mrs Norris, Dickens's Mr and Miss Murdstone, Meredith's Sir Willoughby Patterne, to Samuel Butler's Christina Pontifex, the line runs clear to Ivy Compton-Burnett's families and their fortunes. And all those writers I am sure influenced her. For those who find her novels too highbrow or too feminine or too limited, it may be of interest to know that she expressed to me her enormous respect for and debt to Arnold Bennett's *Old Wives' Tale*; and indeed, Sophia and Constance Povey could be Compton-Burnett names as well as Compton-Burnett characters. But from this great traditional English baron of beef she pared away all the fat of the years, much even of the lean, and then polished the bone until it cleaned and cut and yet was not without essential sweetness. What remains is wit—the wit of Wilde at his best, or Congreve, or, I suspect more influentially, Congreve's great admirer the underestimated Meredith, who in her girlhood was still a literary god; and with the wit, extraordinary wisdom.

She is indeed in her novels an unusual blend of untutored primitivism and exceptional sophistication. Some things, I am sure, she did not do because she could not—she had, for example, no ear for sentence structure or for the euphony of words. Others—descriptions, topicality, analysis, plausibility of action—she rejected quite consciously in favour of what she knew to be essential. So we have her famous dialogues—some spoken, some (but rarely) unspoken, the most half-spoken. This was a form of speech she herself favoured. I remember the sparkle in her deep-set eyes at a restaurant lunch, when a pretentious host kept referring to 'the first-rate minestrone they serve here', and her half-audible 'Oh, I see. Nursery soup!' as she gazed into the sad-looking bowl of brown liquid that the waiter set before her.

To the dialogues she added only short physical descriptions of characters. From these ingredients she constructed with extraordinary skill her wonderful antiphonies of generation—above all in her masterpieces *A Family and a Fortune*, *A House and Its Head*, and *Parents and Children*; the brilliant below-stairs chorus of *Manservant and Maidservant*; or her splendid use of a cat to illustrate human behaviour in *Mother and Son*. These are the

G

highlights of her witty novels with the strict Greek tragic form; these and the strange, powerful sense of money as the corrupter and the solvent of human behaviour that runs through all her books.

She will surely have a high place in English literature—too eccentric to be among the very great, but far too profound to be among the minor. The one danger to her reputation is that, having written so much in a manner so seemingly uniform, her masterpieces may be sucked down among her less-good work and so forgotten. The first task required of serious critics is now that they rescue her from her cultists and proclaim the universality of her best books loudly and clearly to all.

Observer, August 31, 1969

III

Francis King

THERE HAVE ALWAYS been those who have regarded Ivy Compton-Burnett, who died on Wednesday at her home in Kensington, as a freak of English letters: who have complained of the monotony of her settings, of the melodrama of her plots and of the eccentricity of her style.

But to many she was, quite simply, the greatest of living English novelists, with a far profounder understanding of the love of property than Galsworthy and a far deeper insight into sexual motive than D. H. Lawrence.

Her first novel, *Dolores* (1911), was, on her own admission, a false start; her next, *Pastors and Masters* (1925), shows her still unsure how best to use the unique instrument she had fashioned for herself. But from then on she produced novel after novel with little variation of excellence. The apogee of this remarkable career was probably *Manservant and Maidservant*, a novel perfect both in its symmetry and in its balance of comedy and tragedy.

The aphoristic wit of her dialogue has been praised often enough; but no less remarkable are those astonishing aria-like speeches in which her characters reveal, in a language at once formal and passionate, the inmost truth about their complex natures.

Those due to meet her for the first time tended to face the occasion with trepidation. From her writings one might infer a personage as intimidating as Edith Wharton, Edith Sitwell or Virginia Woolf. But in fact few people of her eminence have been more sympathetic to shyness and silliness, more ironically tolerant of pretension and humbug or more lenient to human errors and even vices.

'People are only human,' one of her characters says, adding: 'But it really does not seem much for them to be.' She pitched her own expectations of humanity as low as that aphorism suggests; but despite that fact, her kindness and courtesy were both unfailing.

She was herself a shy woman, and it was no doubt this shyness that earned her the reputation, among people who did not know her well, of being unwilling to talk of anything more momentous than the relative prices of cheddar cheese at Barkers and Harrods. But with a group of people in whose company she felt at her ease, or best of all in a *tête-à-tête*, she was a brilliantly succinct and fascinating talker.

She never wrote a word of literary criticism, but it was with unerring precision that she would indicate the defects in the latest work of this or that admired author of the day. Yet few people whose literary standards were so exacting have found so much to enjoy in even the most ephemeral of books.

Totally without religious belief, she would often say of life: 'It's all we've got.' And this zest for life was the counterpart of her dread of death; so that, even when she was in the greatest pain and discomfort, one never felt, as often with the extremely old and ailing, that the end would be a mercy.

There had been tragedies enough in her family life; but with the same courage that she faced them and drew from them the material of her astonishing novels, she also faced old age and the disabilities and sufferings that came in its train.

She was conscious, as she had every right to be conscious, of the uniqueness of her gifts; and serene in that consciousness, she was wholly free of envy or bitterness about the greater financial success of writers inferior to her.

Going, once, when she had had an accident, to visit her in hospital, I was told by the sister: 'I'm afraid she's been in great pain all today'; but all she herself would say was 'It's not been a good day' before she went on to ask me for news of mutual friends.

She enjoyed reading what others said about her work; but it also amused her when they found in it things of which she had been wholly unaware. 'I suppose that that is what is called *creative* criticism,' she remarked of one such piece.

When infirmity prevented her from going out or moving without difficulty, she saw her friends increasingly at her tea-table. I have a recollection of leaving her there, the last of her guests to depart, and of looking back from the door of the bare, high-ceilinged, darkening room at the tiny figure sitting in-domitably erect before the remains of a nursery tea. 'Do come again soon. I'm always here, you know.'

Yes, she is always there.

Sunday Telegraph, August 31, 1969

The Works of I. ~~nton-Burnett~~

The dates given are ~~...~~ ~~...~~ ication; the
publisher is, in each ~~...~~ nt edition.

Dolores, 1911, Willi~~...~~
Pastors and Masters~~...~~
Brothers and Siste~~...~~
Men and Wives~~...~~
More Women ~~...~~ z Ltd
A House and I~~...~~ Ltd
Daughters and~~...~~ d
A Family and~~...~~ icz Ltd
Parents and C~~...~~ z Ltd
Elders and Be~~...~~ Ltd
Manservant~~...~~ r Gollancz Ltd
Two Worl~~...~~ ctor Gollancz Ltd
Darkness~~...~~ ncz Ltd
The Pres~~...~~ Gollancz Ltd
Mother~~...~~ ncz Ltd
A Fath~~...~~ r Gollancz Ltd
A Her~~...~~ Victor Gollancz Ltd
The~~...~~ , Victor Gollancz Ltd
A G~~...~~ tor Gollancz Ltd
The~~...~~ ictor Gollancz Ltd

C~~...~~ of the novels published 1925–1971,
I~~...~~ Ltd, 1972.

INDEX

BY CHARLES BURKHART